Remote Asylum

by Mart Crowley

A SAMUEL FRENCH ACTING EDITION

SAMUEL FRENCH

FOUNDED 1830

NEW YORK HOLLYWOOD LONDON TORONTO

SAMUELFRENCH.COM

ISBN 978-0-573-60077-7   Printed in U.S.A.   #29734

MUSIC USE NOTE

IMPORTANT BILLING AND CREDIT REQUIREMENTS

REMOTE ASYLUM was first produced by the Center Theater Group, at the Ahmanson Theatre in Los Angeles, California in December, 1970. The performance was directed by Edward Parone, with sets by Ming Cho Lee, costumes by Donald Brooks, lighting by Thomas Skelton. The cast was as follows:

TOM . . . . William Shatner

DINAH . . . . Anne Francis

IRENE . . . . Nancy Kelly

RAY . . . . Arthur O'Connell

MICHAEL . . . . Ralph Williams

CARLOS . . . . Carlos Rivas

JUANITO . . . . Roberto Roberi

GIRL . . . . Annette Cardona

CHARACTERS

TOM – 30, married, All-American Tennis Pro. Tall, handsome, athletic.

DINAH – 30, slim, chic, blonde, ex-actress, ex-wife of a film producer and mother of two children.

MICHAEL – 25, average face, well-groomed, bright, boyish writer.

IRENE – 50-ish, intelligent, imperious, wealthy, well-traveled.

RAY – 60-ish, silver-haired, retired tycoon, terminally ill.

CARLOS – Mid-30s, Hispanic chauffeur/butler, dark, strong, solid.

JUANITO – Mid-20s, androgynous Hispanic servant.

GIRL – Late-teens, silent, innocent, pretty young peasant.

SETTING

A cliff-side mansion on a Mediterranean island.

ABOUT THE SET

The terrace of a "contemporary" mansion, perched high on the coast-line cliff at the most distant point of an unnamed Hispanic island in the Mediterranean [such as Majorca or Ibiza].

Across the width of the stage is the facade of the 1960s-style house, something that suggests a fortress: two multi-floored "towers" at each end, connected by a single-story center section. In the one-level middle portion, there is a big arch leading inside to a foyer in which the front entrance is located [also the unseen side doors to the living and service rooms].

Stage left is the two-story "private tower" – a structure which contains Ray's bedroom suite on the ground floor with an exterior door onto the terrace. Beside Ray's door is a wall niche with a statue of the Virgin Mary. Irene's suite is directly above with an exterior door leading onto a balcony and stairway to the terrace.

Stage right is the "guest tower" – a three level stucco cylinder with suites on each floor, each with doors, balconies and stairways. The ground floor bedroom suite #1, where Tom and Dinah will stay, should be open so action within is visible.

On the left side of the terrace there are wrought iron chairs and a table for dining, and to the right there are chaise longues for sunning. There is a rolling drinks trolley.

Finally, downstage left of the apron there are the "beach stairs" which lead into the orchestra pit.

To Marion Marshall Wagner and Robert John Wagner

ACT I

(Light comes up to reveal the five principals standing at the very extreme of the stage apron, as if on the edge of a precipice. They are looking out over the audience, into space, at what would be the sea.)

(DINAH has on a pants suit and dark glasses and carries a small piece of hand luggage. TOM wears a tennis hat, has a sheathed racquet under his arm and is looking through binoculars. MICHAEL carries a briefcase and a portable Olivetti typewriter. IRENE is in an expensive caftan. RAY is in linen trousers and a sport shirt with the tail hanging out.)

(After a long moment…)

TOM. Faaannn-tastic.

DINAH. Heavenly.

IRENE. *(proudly)* It's something, isn't it?

DINAH. It's heavenly.

IRENE. It's *something!*

TOM. It's fantastic!

IRENE. Well, am I right – or am I right?!

DINAH. *(final, flat)* It's *heavenly,* Irene. *Simply heavenly.*

IRENE. *(not leaving it alone)* Whattaya think, Tom?

TOM. I think it's…fantastic.

IRENE. *(imperiously)* It's like Dinah says – it's *heavenly.* Like heaven. *(to RAY)* – Isn't it, my darling?

(goes to RAY, cuddles, kisses him)

What does my baby think? Hmmm?

(RAY mouths some indistinguishable words…)

DINAH. *(turns to* **MICHAEL***)* And what do you think, Signor Silencio?

MICHAEL. I think we've *done* the *view.*

IRENE. *(breaks from* **RAY***)* What did you say?

MICHAEL. *(deferentially dry)* I think it's something like *you:* a bit of heaven – like Dinah says.

IRENE. You bet it is! Right, Tom?

TOM. It's fannnnnn-fuckin'-tastic, sweetheart! Like Michael says – like *you!*

(**TOM** *throws his arms about* **IRENE,** *lifts her, kisses her on the cheek…*)

DINAH. *(lightly disapproving) Honnn*eeee!

IRENE. *(squeals of mock protest)* Taaahhhmmmmmm! Such *language!* You're a scandal!

TOM. *(smooth charm)* Lady, you are something else!

(**TOM** *puts* **IRENE** *down, slaps her lightly on the rear.* **IRENE** *shrieks gleefully.*)

DINAH. *(to no one)* Honestly.

IRENE. *(coy young girl)* Ray, did you see what Tom did to your mama?!

(**TOM** *picks up* **IRENE** *again and swings her around.*)

(louder squeal, more protestation) Ohh! Oh, Tom, now, stop! Put me down! Ray, make him put me down! Raa-aayeee! *(giggles)* Ohh…I'm so dizzy. I'm so dizzzeeeeee!

(**RAY** *starts to chuckle.* **DINAH** *turns to observe* **RAY***'s private mocking laugh.*)

DINAH. *(without effort)* That's enough, Tom.

(**RAY** *laughs more and more.* **TOM** *releases* **IRENE** *as she becomes aware of* **RAY***…*)

IRENE. *(catching breath, to* **RAY***)* Ohh, my darling! You're laughing! It's so wonderful to hear you laugh again! *(a beat)* You're not laughing at me, are you? Well, I don't care!

*(rushes to **RAY**, puts her arms about him)*

IRENE. Tom! Tom, you've made Ray laugh again! Oh, thank God you're here! – *(goes to **DINAH**)* Dinah, my dear…how can I ever thank you for coming?

DINAH. *(evenly)* We're thankful to be here, too. You have no idea.

TOM. We all need a rest, Irene. We need to get away. We're tired.

DINAH. Bone tired. And I don't mean from the flight.

TOM. *(a weak wing with his racquet)* I'm afraid we're rather played-out. Pun intended. It's the end of the tour.

MICHAEL. *(to himself)* The *edge* of the world. *(lightly)* It's only the end of the *map! (moves to lip of apron)* As far as one can go. One more step and you're over the hill. One false step and it's man overboard!

IRENE. Young man, what are you trying to say?!

MICHAEL. I'm saying what I'm saying.

IRENE. Then what you are saying sounds morbid and this place is utterly *sans souci*! This place is *something*! And this is out-of season!

MICHAEL. *(wipes his brow)* You're telling *me!*

IRENE. That's why we retired here – to get away from it all!

MICHAEL. "Retired." Now that sounds morbid.

IRENE. *(sardonically, to **DINAH** and **TOM**)* Who is this charming friend of yours?

TOM. Michael's an old friend of *mine.*

DINAH. And now mine. We ran into him in Rome and he's been traveling with us since. We've become really quite attached. *(puts her arm about **MICHAEL**)* Haven't we, kiddo?

MICHAEL. *(sweetly)* I love you, Dinah. You've saved my life. I hope that's what I wanted.

*(**DINAH** strokes **MICHAEL**'s hair, but he moves away, wanders off to himself.)*

IRENE. *(re: Michael)* What an odd duck.

DINAH. *(to* **IRENE***)* When he drinks too much he's like a child.

IRENE. *(bluntly)* You don't need any more children.

(**RAY** *turns away, watches* **MICHAEL.***)*

DINAH. *(flatly, to* **IRENE***)* I need the ones I have.

(**RAY** *turns back to* **DINAH***, gasps a few words.)*

Yes, Ray? – (**RAY** *mouths something.)* The kids? How are my kids? *(***RAY** *nods.)* Just great. They're with their father in the south of France. He gets them for six weeks in the summer.

IRENE. *(sarcastically)* And did you see dear Jerry?

DINAH. No, he sent a car and driver to Nice to collect the kids. Tom was in a tournament in Monte Carlo.

IRENE. *(disdainfully)* My, my, living the high life in Beverly Hills and the Cote D'Azur! Jerry's come a long way for a cheap theatrical promoter.

DINAH. I admit he was always a bit grand, Irene. But cheap, *never!* And believe me, it sickens me to defend him. *(to* **RAY***)* What, luv?

(**RAY** *leads her to some measures scratched on the wall of the house.)*

DINAH. *(laughs)* Oh, no, they've grown since then! *(indicates on wall)* They're up to here now. Two little bean poles! *(to* **TOM***)* Look, darling, the marks Ray made when the boys were here with me the last time.

TOM. Jesus, they *have* taken off!

(**RAY** *taps another marking.)*

DINAH. Yes, Ray, I see the date. God, how time flies-even when you're *not* having a good time. *(to* **TOM***)* Jerry and I had just separated.

TOM. But, Ray, you saw the kids at Christmas!

IRENE. He remembers very little from that ghastly trip.

TOM. *(to* **RAY***)* You remember meeting me, don't you?

(**RAY** *nods.)*

DINAH. *(to* RAY*)* How's your daughter?

 *(*RAY *looks down.)*

IRENE. *(snaps)* We never see her.

DINAH. I'd die if I didn't see my children.

IRENE. No, you wouldn't.

DINAH. Oh, but I would. If I didn't have my kids, I wouldn't have anything to live for.

IRENE. You have Tom. He's all you need. And you know what, you don't even really need him. I'm sorry, Tom, but I have to say it: Dinah's too independent to need *anybody*. Dinah, you're like me.

DINAH. No, I'm not, Irene.

IRENE. *(going right ahead)* I never wanted children, but if I had, I'd have liked to have a *daughter* like you, Dinah.

MICHAEL. *(to* IRENE*)* But I thought you said you *have* a daughter.

IRENE. She's Ray's. By his first marriage. *(changing subject)* How long is it from Nice these days?

DINAH. Oh, I don't know. We went from Nice to Madrid to…

MICHAEL. *(turns)* I'd say it's about a two-martini flight. To Madrid. One and a half from there.

IRENE. *(to* DINAH *and* TOM*)* Would you like something cool to drink?

TOM. Beautiful.

IRENE. Some lemonade?

MICHAEL. *Lemonade?!*

IRENE. I'm sure you want to bathe and lie down a while…?

DINAH. *(exhausted)* That would be heavenly – just to rest.

 *(*IRENE *indicates a bar cart…)*

IRENE. *(to* TOM*)* Make yourself at home.

TOM. *(Goes to bar. To* MICHAEL*)* Swifty?

MICHAEL. I'm not sure our hostess approves. Or, maybe I should say, approves of *me*.

IRENE. Any friend of Dinah's…

MICHAEL. …had better watch their step with you.

(DINAH *laughs*.)

IRENE. *(to* DINAH, *laughs)* Such *insolence!* I'm not at all sure I like your friend.

DINAH. *(good-naturedly)* You will. When you met Tom at Christmas you didn't exactly think he was off the top of the tree.

IRENE. Nonsense! I *adored* Tom from the moment you introduced us!

DINAH. No, you didn't.

MICHAEL. *(to* IRENE, *re:* DINAH) Dinah tells the truth. And she's not going to let you do otherwise.

TOM. That's right. She'll nail you.

IRENE. *(laughs)* That's right, Dinah. I didn't.

(TOM *moves away from bar.* MICHAEL's *expression slides…)*

TOM. *(insecurely)* You didn't like me?

IRENE. Couldn't you tell?

TOM. No.

DINAH. He could tell. *(to* TOM) Tell the truth. You had to work a little harder than usual to win Irene over.

TOM. *(with an edge)* Game, set and match to you, kiddo.

IRENE. Shhhh! Listen!

TOM. What, Irene?

IRENE. *SHHHH!*

(*a beat. Silence*)

I heard it! Didn't you? Didn't you hear it?!

DINAH. Hear what, Irene?

IRENE. A baby. A baby, crying. Sometimes it sounds far away. Sometimes…not so far. Surely you heard it!

DINAH. No.

IRENE. Tom?

TOM. *(shrugs)* Sorry.

MICHAEL. *(a mocking sound)* Waaaa-a-a-a!

> *(**RAY** chuckles. **IRENE** turns to glare at **MICHAEL**.)*

> *(to **IRENE**, re: drink)* Sometimes when I don't get my bottle, I cry like a baby.

IRENE. Help yourself! - Put a nipple on it, if you like.

> *(**MICHAEL** goes to bar, fixes a drink. **RAY** continues to laugh. **IRENE** goes to him.)*

> *(to **RAY**)* Ray, you heard it this time, didn't you? Didn't you, my darling?

> *(**RAY** laughs, a bit out of control.)*

Ray! Answer me! Stop that laughing! You'll have a heart attack right here in the middle of this million-dollar terrazzo!

> *(**RAY** stops laughing.)*

Did you hear the crying? The baby?

> *(He shakes his head.)*

Are you telling me the truth? I don't think you're telling me the truth!

> *(**DINAH** turns away.)*

> *(hears something)* SHHHHHHHH! LISTEN!

MICHAEL. *(sipping his drink)* No one is talking but you, Irene.

IRENE. Quiet! I hear something! *(Silence. A beat)* No, it's only your luggage.

> *(**JUANITO**, a thin manservant with plucked eyebrows, dressed in tight jeans, a white house jacket and too much gold jewelry, chains, ear-ring and bracelets, stumbles onto the terrace, struggling with various "good" suitcases. He's angrily mumbling to himself in Spanish, idiosyncratic of Majorca or Ibiza. He drops the bags, kicks them, spewing vulgar slang.)*

> *(crossing)* Juanito! Stop that! *(heavy American accent)* Paren, me oyen?!

(JUANITO *kicks the bags and screams epithets.*)

IRENE. *(cont.)* Paren! *He dicho paren!*

(CARLOS *enters, dressed in a black suit and chauffeur's cap, carrying some more luggage under his arms.*)

CARLOS. *(coolly authoritative)* Basta!

(JUANITO *calms.* IRENE *eyes* CARLOS *disdainfully.*)

IRENE. Just who's giving the orders around here?!

MICHAEL. Good question.

IRENE. *(ignores remark)* Cargen estas maletas! *(to* DINAH*)* – You and Tom will have your old room. *(to* JUANITO*)* Apartemento uno para la senora y el senor. *(to* CARLOS, *re* MICHAEL*)* El dos para el amigo del senor.

JUANITO. *(taunting* CARLOS*)* Y el tres?

CARLOS. *(strikes* JUANITO*)* Silencio!

IRENE. *(to* CARLOS*)* How *dare* you! Ray, there's another example of this man's insubordination. I tell you, Carlos must be fired!

(RAY *panics, rushes to her, gasping protest.*)

(restraining RAY*)* Now, now, calm down! You mustn't excite yourself so! Ray! Please!

(RAY *continues hysterically until* CARLOS *goes to him.*)

CARLOS. Senor! Por favor calmense. Por favor a mi.

IRENE. *(to* CARLOS*)* TAKE YOUR HANDS OFF HIM!

(RAY *calms.*)

Dejalo, vete!

(CARLOS *backs away.*)

Ray, don't excite yourself with this. I'll deal with them later. Luego! Me ocupare de ustedes mas tardes. Vayanse!

(JUANITO *fingers his gold chains, sucks a tooth, picks up the scattered luggage and goes into the ground floor guest suite # 1.* CARLOS *looks toward* RAY, *nods slightly.* RAY *responds, sees* IRENE *catch him, turns away.*)

IRENE. *(cont.)* *(to* **CARLOS***) He dicho, vayanse!*

> *(***CARLOS*** *climbs the exterior stairs and goes into guest apartment #2.* **IRENE** *crosses to* **RAY***.)*

Sweetheart, what did Carlos nod to you about? Something is going on behind my back, isn't it?

> *(***RAY*** *shakes his head as* **CARLOS** *comes out of guest suite #2, checks* **IRENE***, then quietly goes up to enter #3.)*

DINAH. *(to* **MICHAEL***)* I didn't know you spoke Spanish.

MICHAEL. I don't, but I get the drift.

DINAH. *(smiles)* All that Latin as an altar boy finally coming in handy.

MICHAEL. That's not exactly what I meant.

IRENE. *(warming a bit to* **MICHAEL***)* Ray was raised a Catholic. He left the church when he divorced his first wife for me, but he's still devout. I had the architect who did this house design that niche over there for him. He never misses Mass on Sunday. You can go with him.

> *(***RAY*** *looks expectantly toward* **MICHAEL**…*)*

MICHAEL. Well, I don't think… *(sees how much it means to* **RAY***)* Yes, sir. I'll go with you.

> *(***RAY*** *takes* **MICHAEL***'s hand, smiles.)*

IRENE. I have no religion myself but I'm glad Ray has his faith. It's a source of great solace to him and for that, I'm grateful. Human beings need something to grasp onto in trying times – and I'm for anything that works. *(crosses, puts her arms about* **RAY***)* It's way past Ray's nap time. It's time we all had a siesta. A nice, long, long rest.

DINAH. Heavenly.

IRENE. Dinah, you know the way. *(wryly)* Why don't you lead your…charges. After you've bathed and had a lie-down – cocktails here on the terrace. And then, I'll take you off to a party.

TOM. Fantastic.

IRENE. Our neighbor across the bay is having a little fiesta this evening and we're all invited. *(to* **RAY***)* Come along, my darling, it's beddie-bye for you! *(reacts to something)* Ohhh! Lucky is gone! *(to* **TOM***)* Didn't you see the dog lying here?

TOM. As a matter of fact, I didn't.

IRENE. I chained him here myself *(to* **MICHAEL***)* Didn't you see him?

MICHAEL. I'm a bad one to ask. Sometime I see all sorts of creatures.

DINAH. You take too many pills.

IRENE. *(exasperated)* Ray, you didn't let Lucky go again, did you? *(***RAY** *shakes his head.)* Now, don't tell me you didn't when I know you did!

*(***RAY** *chuckles, crosses to the bar, lifts a bottle of Scotch.* **IRENE** *darts after him.)*

No, no, no! Bad boy! *(takes the bottle away)* You know the doctor said only one before dinner. Now, come on- everybody off to bed! *(catches herself)* To *nap.* Everybody off *to nap!*

*(***DINAH** *and* **TOM** *cross to their suite #1 and enter.* **MICHAEL** *climbs the stairs to his quarters #2, hesitates to observe* **IRENE** *and* **RAY** *below…)*

Ray, wait! *(vulnerable, girlish)* – Why…why did you laugh when Tom slapped Irene on her tush? Huh? You weren't laughing *at* her, were you? *(no answer from* **RAY***)* Say, "no." Please…say, "no."

(Finally, **RAY** *shakes his head, walks off.)*

I didn't think you would. I knew you weren't laughing at…*me.*

*(***RAY** *goes to his room off the terrace, shuts the door.* **IRENE** *slowly climbs to her own quarters, goes inside.* **MICHAEL** *then turns and enters the guest suite #2. The stage is empty. A beat. There is the sound of a baby's cry. Momentarily,* **CARLOS** *exits the "unoccupied" guest suite #3. He quickly descends all the way to the beach*

stairs. He whistles and momentarily, Lucky, the German Shepherd comes up. **CARLOS** *pats him on the head and quietly whispers to the dog in Spanish.* **CARLOS** *quickly crosses to the bar, retrieves the bottle of Scotch and goes to* **RAY***'s door, knocks gently.* **RAY** *opens the door, pats the dog and accepts the whiskey.* **CARLOS** *quickly recloses the door and exits through the foyer arch. Lights come up in guest suite #1.* **TOM** *is twirling his tennis racket.* **DINAH** *is sitting on the bed, talking on the phone.)*

DINAH. *(into phone)* When will they be back? Quand seront-ils la? Is there anyone there who speaks English? Where's the children's governess? *(to* **TOM***)* Gone, too. And Jerry didn't say where he was taking them. I don't understand this. *(into the phone)* Allo? Ou sont-ils alles? Priez de m'appeler a ce numero. Merci. *(Hangs up. To* **TOM***)* Something's wrong. I know it. I just know it.

TOM. *(unconcerned)* You sound like Irene.

DINAH. Paranoid?

TOM. *(wearily)* The kids are okay, Dinah.

*(**DINAH** gets up, takes off her shoes, slacks and blouse, hangs them neatly.)*

DINAH. I'm not worried about them, exactly. I mean, about their *safety* or anything like that. *(directly)* I know they're "okay," thank you very much. It's not that.

TOM. It's Jerry. He's what's eating you.

DINAH. I wouldn't trust that son-of-a-bitch with the key to a can of sardines. Let alone with my...with my babies.

TOM. Relax. Seven and nine...they're not exactly babies anymore. They can take care of themselves.

DINAH. *(somewhat proudly)* Yeah. They're tough, those kids. *(locks eyes with* **TOM***)* I know what you're thinking. Go ahead and say it: "Tough like their mother."

TOM. *(turns away)* I wasn't thinking that. *You* were thinking that.

*(**DINAH**, barefoot, in her bra and panties, slips into a man's pajama top.)*

DINAH. Okay. What *were* you thinking? You seem even farther away than usual.

TOM. *(unbuttoning shirt)* I was wondering what you're gonna do when they grow-up and leave you.

DINAH. *(after a moment)* Try to be realistic. Let go.

*(***TOM*** *drops his shirt on a chair, slips off his pants, throws them on the chair.)*

TOM. I hope you can manage it when the time comes to let go.

DINAH. *(meaningfully)* And it's only a matter of time, isn't it?

TOM. *(evasively)* It's good they're with Jerry. They need a father.

DINAH. *(pointedly)* Don't you think *I* know that?

TOM. I'll give *you* a break if you'll give *me* a break.

DINAH. Jerry doesn't give a damn about those kids. It's *my* scalp he wants. He's just using them to get to me, and I know he's up to something. I know too well the way that bastard's mind works!

TOM. Alright, for Christ's sake! I don't wanna hear anymore about Jerry *or* the kids! It was a deal, remember? That's why we're here-to get away from it all - all of them, once and for all - or, at least, for a little while, right?

DINAH. *(calmly)* And Karen, included.

TOM. *(finally)* And Karen included.

*(***TOM*** *shakes his head, bounces the tennis ball with the racquet, catches the ball fiercely.)*

Couldn't resist, could you?!

DINAH. I'm sorry. I'm jealous, I admit it. I'm not proud of it, but there it is.

(There is a loud offstage crash of dishware, followed by a heated, indistinguishable exchange in Spanish.)

TOM. This place is like some kind of loonie bin.

DINAH. I said I'd come alone. I warned you.

TOM. *(twirls his racquet)* What makes me think anything'll be different anywhere else? What makes me think with a passport and a plane ticket the pasture's any greener?

(Another crash offstage. **IRENE**'s *door opens. She comes down the stairs to enter the house.)*

Jesus, I don't know if I can take it here!

DINAH. Give it a chance.

TOM. *(after a moment)* I *want* to stop running. Honest I do.

DINAH. If it doesn't work out, we can cut it short. She's afraid he's going to die and leave her all alone. I can understand that. That's why I had to come.

TOM. What made me think anything would be better here? Nothing is any different. The kids are still with us. Your husband is still with us.

DINAH. And your wife is still with us. And your *life* is still with you. No matter how far or how fast you travel.

TOM. *(lightly)* Get off my back.

(Another crash followed by more garbled yelling from **IRENE** *in terrible Spanish.)*

DINAH. You think I don't know why you keep Michael around? As a pipeline to Karen.

TOM. *(exhausted)* Get…off…my…back!

(A final crash. Silence. A beat…)

DINAH. Go on, go! To Rio or Rangoon or wherever you can smash a ball over a net and pull the wool over your baby blue eyes!

TOM. I can't go another step. Something inside me is broken in two.

DINAH. Then stay with me! *(crossing to* **TOM***)* I can put you back together, Humpty-Dumpty. I'm good at that, aren't I?

TOM. *(puts his hand on her breast)* Are you…are you too tired?

DINAH. *(directly)* Not if you mean it.

TOM. *(turns away)* What the hell is that? I always mean it. Don't I?

DINAH. *(coolly) You* tell *me.*

TOM. *(viciously)* FUCK OFF!

DINAH. That's more like it. Direct contact. That wasn't so hard, now was it?

(**TOM** *turns and slaps* **DINAH.**)

TOM. *(instantly)* I'm sorry.

DINAH. *(smoothes her hair)* Your backhand's as strong as ever.

(**TOM** *turns away, looks out the door at the sea.* **DINAH** *takes a deck of cards from her handbag, starts to play solitaire on the bed. The door to* **RAY**'s *room opens. He exits to return the partially depleted Scotch bottle to the bar.* **IRENE** *can once again be heard babbling away in Spanish, her chatter punctuated with exclamations of "Carlos! Carlos!"* **MICHAEL** *comes out onto his balcony, observes* **RAY** *straightening the liquor bottles.* **IRENE** *is heard approaching.* **RAY** *quickly returns to his room, closing his door.* **MICHAEL** *quickly comes down to the bar, pours another vodka.* **IRENE**'s *voice loudens.* **MICHAEL** *straightens the bottles, heads for his room but doesn't have time to make it and hides behind a potted palm.* **IRENE** *bursts upon the terrace, followed by* **JUANITO.**)

IRENE. Carlos! Carlos!

JUANITO. *(indicating* **CARLOS** *has gone)* Desaparecio.

IRENE. Yes, well, he *will* be gone! I can assure you that! By sundown! *(spots liquor bottles)* ¿Que pasa aqui? ¿Quien has estado tomando esta bebida? *(picks up Scotch)* I measured and marked this bottle this morning! Now, look! *(sees vodka bottle)* And the vodka! Ray doesn't even drink vodka! *(picks it up)* Mira! If I didn't know better I'd think you're turning into a lush! ¿Quien se has tomando esto?

JUANITO. *(shakes his head)* No se, Senora.

IRENE. ¡Dime!

JUANITO. *(indicates* **RAY**'s *room)* Carlos le da whiskey a Senor.

IRENE. Lock up the bottles and give me the key! Encierren estas botellas…

JUANITO. Yeah, yeah, Senora.

(IRENE crosses to RAY's door, knocks gently.)

IRENE. Ray, are you asleep? Ray, I have to talk to you. *(opens door, peeks inside)* Are you taking a nap, my darling? *(a beat)* Ray…do you drink behind my back? Does Carlos give you whiskey behind my back?

(No response. She closes the door.)

– I'm sorry. Get your rest. I'm sorry. *(sees JUANITO watching her…)* Well, go on! Vayanse!

(JUANITO goes to the bar cart, starts to push it away. IRENE goes up the steps to her balcony, goes inside her room. JUANITO stops, puts his hand on his hips, starts to mimic IRENE, prancing and cackling low in Spanish with an American accent. MICHAEL steps out from behind the plant. JUANITO turns to see MICHAEL and freezes, somewhat panic-stricken at first. Then, his attitude changes to one of hauteur and defiance as he pointedly snatches the vodka bottle from the bar, puts it under his arm and rolls the trolley away. MICHAEL, drink in hand, goes to DINAH and TOM's room, knocks.)

MICHAEL. It's Michael. Can I come in?

DINAH. It's open.

(MICHAEL enters. DINAH continues to play cards on her side of the bed. TOM is propped on pillows on his side, under the covers. He is smoking, his tennis hat pushed down over his eyes.)

(not looking up) Well, how do you like it so far?

MICHAEL. *About your friends. And* their retinue.

DINAH. Perfect, aren't they?

MICHAEL. The original Dynamic Duo. Rather, she's the original Dynamic Duo. He's The Invisible Man.

TOM. She's chopped off his balls and stuffed 'em in his mouth so that poor son-of-a-bitch can't even say "Uncle!"

MICHAEL. *(sardonically, re: Tom)* He's cute, Dinah! Why don't you marry him?

TOM. *(to MICHAEL)* Shut up and sit down.

DINAH. I already married one asshole, what do I need with another? *(to TOM, re: his remark about IRENE)* That's not really fair. She didn't personally give him cancer. Someone had to take charge.

MICHAEL. Coming to this quaint little haven has not, thus far, been the orgy of tranquility we anticipated, am I correct?

TOM. What the hell do you care? You found the booze to wash down whatever shit you're taking, didn't you?

DINAH. *(casually)* Tom may leave. You go with him. I'll catch up.

MICHAEL. *(sloshes his drink)* Leave?! Before we know the answer to the riddle of "The Baby?"

TOM. *(sliding down in bed, pulling up covers)* We're a little late folks, so g'night!

DINAH. *(to MICHAEL, re: drink)* You're gonna be in great shape by dinner.

MICHAEL. Listen, I know you think I hear voices, but I did hear a baby cry. Who's locked in the attic? Ray's mad illegitimate child by the first wife?

TOM. You better lay off that shit.

MICHAEL. I've only had one drink and a valium. Don't you think that's fair? One *stolen* drink. A multi-million dollar layout like this and you have to cop a drink! Irene had her bangling, jangling, clanging amigo lock up the liquor. (**MICHAEL** *sits on the foot of the bed.)*

TOM. Pills and likker – stops your ticker.

DINAH. *(to MICHAEL)* Listen, kiddo, will you please not knock my cards to hell and gone?

TOM. *(to MICHAEL, over his shoulder)* Go to your room. You've had too much Christmas.

MICHAEL. *(to DINAH and TOM)* Can I get in bed with you?

TOM. It looks like you're already *in* bed with us.

MICHAEL. I mean under the covers. Even though it's sunny, I'm cold.

DINAH. Oh, honestly, Michael, you're worse than a two year-old! Okay! Get in!

MICHAEL. Oh, goody, goody!

DINAH. Watch out, don't spill that martini!

(**MICHAEL** *quickly crawls to the middle of the king-size bed, gets under the covers between them.*)

MICHAEL. Ohh, this is fun! Here we are, all snuggled up, cozy and warm.

TOM. *(turns away)* Jesus Christ! I don't believe this!

MICHAEL. Here we are in our house – we've made a little house for ourselves all cozy and warm and nothing can hurt us.

(**DINAH** *starts to laugh out loud.* **TOM** *pushes up on his arm, turns to look at* **DINAH**.)

TOM. *(to DINAH)* Are you ready for this crazy bastard? Is he beautiful?!

DINAH. *(stops laughing)* Honestly. Do you have any idea how many times a day you say "fantastic" and "beautiful"?

TOM. Honestly, do you have any idea how many times you say "honestly"?

MICHAEL. Don't fight. Please don't fight.

DINAH. *(to MICHAEL, re: Tom)* Hit him for me, will you?

TOM. Get off my back!

DINAH. That's another one!

MICHAEL. Please, please don't fight!

TOM. Nobody's fighting! Don't get hysterical!

MICHAEL. Sometimes I think you all fight just so you can have a fabulous reconciliation fuck.

(*A beat.* **DINAH** *bursts out with a loud laugh.*)

TOM. *(loud hoot)* Whoo-hooo! Oh, Jesus, Cuckoo City!

(**TOM** *starts to laugh, slap the bed.* **MICHAEL** *spills some of his drink on* **DINAH**. *She screams, then laughs heartily…*)

DINAH. Ohh! I told you not to spill that fucking drink! Shit, I'm all wet!

TOM. *(laughs)* Yeah, I'll say you're all wet!

DINAH. What're *you* laughing at?

TOM. You!

DINAH. You should see yourself in that stupid hat!

*(**TOM** gives her the Bronx cheer. She dips her fingers in **MICHAEL**'s drink, flicks it in **TOM**'s face.)*

MICHAEL. Hey! What makes you think I want somebody's fingers up my drink!

*(**TOM** takes the glass from **MICHAEL**, pours it over his head. **MICHAEL** lets off a shriek, they all collapse with laughter as the phone rings.)*

DINAH. *(seriously)* It's the phone! Maybe it's the kids! Michael, gimme the phone! Quick, baby!

*(**MICHAEL** reaches over **TOM** to answer the phone on the night table.)*

MICHAEL. *(into phone)* Bellevue. Isolation ward. Just a minute. *(hands **DINAH** receiver)* It's the head matron.

DINAH. *(disappointed)* Oh. *(brightly, into phone)* Yes, Irene? Ohh, the boys were just…cutting up.

MICHAEL. *(cups hands megaphone style)* Cutting up before we cut out!

DINAH. *(covering receiver)* Honeee!

*(**TOM** pops **MICHAEL** on the head.)*

MICHAEL. OW!

TOM. What's the matter, boy, have you lost your marbles?

MICHAEL. *(singing with Castilian "lisp" to* "I Left My Heart in San Francisco"*)* "I los-th my mind…th-outh of Ibi-tha"

TOM. *(mimicking **IRENE**)* Don't be insolent. I'm not certain I like you.

*(**TOM** and **MICHAEL** continue to giggle.)*

DINAH. *(into phone)* Yes, Irene. I'll come over.

DINAH. *(hangs up phone)* Honestly, you two!

MICHAEL. What was that all about?

TOM. Orders from headquarters.

(DINAH gets up, straightens her hair, slips on a robe.)

DINAH. Listen, if there're any long distance calls, I'll be with the head honcho.

(She exits. They stop laughing. MICHAEL moves over to DINAH's side of the bed.)

TOM. Shit, man, what am I doing here? What am I doing in this cracker factory at the end of…

MICHAEL. …the line.

TOM. What?

MICHAEL. Rope. The end of our rope.

TOM. *(reflectively)* Man, I am so fucked-up. Like you wouldn't believe!

MICHAEL. I would believe.

(DINAH pauses when she sees RAY's door open. She watches as RAY comes out unsteadily, leading the German Shepherd to the beach stairs, where he releases the animal. RAY crosses back to the niche, attempts to kneel, but stumbles, fails. DINAH rushes to help him.)

DINAH. *(to RAY)* It's all right, dear. It's only me.

(RAY looks at her, dazed. He finally smiles, as if he recognizes her. She helps him to his feet, leads him back inside his room.)

TOM. *(to MICHAEL)* I can't tell you what it's been like to have you to talk to. Better than paying a psychiatrist.

MICHAEL. Costs about the same, having me around to listen. Maybe I'm a little cheaper. No comments, please.

TOM. I still win some pretty good purses – make a pretty good living, but…how much longer can I hold out?

MICHAEL. Actually, you don't pay me to listen. You pay me to talk. To tell you Karen stories.

TOM. Listen, Swifty, level with me. You think it's serious between her and that "king of the schlubs" or whatever it is he calls himself?

MICHAEL. The Shoe King of the Suburbs – *please*. He has an ad on TV.

TOM. Tell me the truth. How serious is it?

MICHAEL. What do I know?! How serious is it between you and Dinah? Well, make that, "How serious are *you?*"

TOM. *(anxiously evasive)* Oh, Christ, I don't want to think about that! I'm getting in deeper and deeper and I don't know how to get out before it's too late. Man, I've gotten myself in the biggest fuckin' trap. And I've got to get out. Now. Fast. Before it's too late.

MICHAEL. Tom, I think she really loves you.

TOM. Karen?

MICHAEL. *Dinah!*

TOM. *(deflates)* Oh. Listen, let's call Karen and tell her we're coming back. Both of us. That we're on our way home – whatta ya say?

*(He reaches for the phone. **MICHAEL** stops him.)*

MICHAEL. Tom – make sense. Things have changed. Karen's the one to come back if any coming-back's to be done. She's the one who walked out on you. You can't go back to something that's not there to go back to.

TOM. Swifty, I know we're going to get back together. I just *know* we are! Let's call her now! She'd get a kick out of hearing from both of us. Did she know you were going to meet me?

MICHAEL. No.

TOM. Where would she be, huh? What time is it there now?

MICHAEL. *(warningly)* Tom. *Don't!*

TOM. Tell me where she is!

MICHAEL. *(after a moment)* At *his* place.

TOM. Oh. Well. You know what the number is, don't you?

*(**MICHAEL** nods. **TOM** picks up the phone.)*

How do you get Long Distance?

(DINAH exits RAY's room and crosses to the "private" tower stairs as IRENE comes out of her room.)

IRENE. Dinah, darling?

DINAH. Yes, Irene?

IRENE. Come up, come up! What took you so long?

DINAH. I was just...I was hoping maybe I'd hear from the kids. I have a call into them. I was waiting for them to call back.

IRENE. *(settles on a chaise longue)* Come sit with me. Here beside me.

(DINAH sits beside IRENE.)

Take this pillow and put it behind your back. There. Isn't that better? Aren't you comfortable?

DINAH. *(puts pillow behind her)* Thank you.

IRENE. I can't tell you what a comfort it is for me to have you here. These last weeks have been...would you like a drink?

DINAH. Nothing. Thank you.

IRENE. I have anything you want in my room. White wine, whiskey, anything.

DINAH. I don't want anything.

IRENE. *(gets up)* Maybe some sherry. I generally have some sherry this time of the afternoon. Or a glass of champagne. Only that which comes from the grape. *(IRENE goes into her room.)*

DINAH. Nothing, really. Thank you.

IRENE. *(returns with sherry)* I never take anything that does not come from the grape. You don't really drink, do you?

DINAH. Not really.

IRENE. Neither do I, really. But this is quite good this time of day. *(pours Dinah a glass)* Here. Take it. I know you don't really want it, but I want you to try it.

DINAH. *(takes glass, tries a sip)* Thank you.

IRENE. Like it?

DINAH. It's very nice.

IRENE. *(sits beside* **DINAH***)* I knew you'd like it. It's local. Are you comfortable?

DINAH. Yes.

IRENE. *(takes* **DINAH***'s hand)* I can't tell you what a strain I've been under. How can I ever repay you for coming?

DINAH. Please, Irene. I don't want anything from you.

IRENE. I cannot believe that in life people can ever not want anything from anyone. But, Dinah, I believe *you.* I usually don't like women at all. But with you, I don't feel threatened by your friendship.

DINAH. What an odd thing to say. Threatened?

IRENE. We're all feeding off each other, my dear. Taking little bites out of each other. It's a universal condition. But you're different. I actually believe you are unselfish. Are you sure you're comfortable?

DINAH. Well…

IRENE. *I'm* not really comfortable. *(gets up)* Come on, take your sherry and come with me. *(moves across her balcony)* Ah, look at that sky! Just look at the colors in that sky!

*(***DINAH*** *follows* ***IRENE*** *onto the center portion of the house over the foyer. They are now bathed in rays of pink and orange and magenta.)*

DINAH. It's heavenly, Irene.

IRENE. It's overwhelming. It makes one aware of so many things that are unanswerable.

*(***RAY*** *moans in his sleep.)*

Life. Limitation. Limitlessness. It makes one stop and take stock. Do you ever think about God, Dinah?

DINAH. Not much.

IRENE. Do you think there is one?

DINAH. I don't know.

IRENE. What do you think happens to us after we die?

DINAH. Personally, I don't think anything happens to us. I think it's over. I just think that's it. Peace. At last.

(a beat)

IRENE. Ray is dying, Dinah.

DINAH. I know.

IRENE. That's why I asked you to come here. *Ray is dying.*

DINAH. Well, Irene, forgive me if I sound glib – that's one thing we all have to do.

IRENE. *(laughs)* You have such a remarkably simple way of looking at things.

DINAH. I just don't think there's any point wasting any time with things which cannot be changed or helped. I have as many short-comings and insecurities as anybody else. I feel as though it's a never ending battle to stay just this side of insanity – to not slip over the edge. I think...I hope that no matter the problem, I can deal with it without losing my footing. I think...I don't want to believe...I could go crazy over any*thing*...or any*one*.

IRENE. I envy you.

DINAH. Don't envy me. Of anything. I'm as scared as the next one.

IRENE. Could you stand it if Tom left?

DINAH. I don't know. I guess I'd find out. He may very well- any day. I think eventually, he will.

IRENE. And when your children grow up and leave you? And they will.

DINAH. That's a fact of life. It simply *is* the way it is. And if I cannot live with it – I will, quite simply, die.

(RAY moans.)

IRENE. What am I going to do when Ray dies?

DINAH. You'll go on. You'll be the same...until you die. The only thing that will change when Ray dies is that he won't be here anymore.

IRENE. *(vulnerably)* Oh, Dinah I'm...I'm terrified of being left alone. When Ray dies will you come and live here with me?

DINAH. I don't see how that would be realistic.

IRENE. I'm *panicked,* Dinah, that at my age I won't ever again find anyone! I'm not so old. I'm not so ugly – am I? Oh, it's cruel. The desire is still there, but look at me. That's cruel.

DINAH. Your looks are fine for a woman your age. And what does it matter? It all goes, finally. For all of us – male and female. No one, these days, knows better than I, that when something is over, *it is over.*

IRENE. Please, please don't leave, Dinah. I beg you.

DINAH. You helped me, Irene – once, when I was alone after Jerry and I broke up. That's why I came to you now – and, selfishly, I suppose, to take advantage of your lovely refuge and rest a while. I'm so exhausted from trying to stay on top of things. Stay one step ahead. But I'm losing ground, now. I'm losing my… *(DINAH sags a bit.)*

IRENE. I know. I know what you mean, my dear. And you couldn't have come to a better place. Come with me. Give me your hand. *(leads DINAH to her bedroom)* Rest inside. Lie down on my bed and rest. Stay here in my room. Stay as long as you like.

(IRENE leads DINAH into her room. TOM snores inside suite #1. MICHAEL covers him with a sheet, quietly gets out of bed and wanders out onto the terrace, starts up to his own room, suite #2, in the guest tower.)

(Suddenly, there is the sound of a baby crying. MICHAEL races up the stairs to suite #3, and goes inside.)

(IRENE comes out of her room, listens. RAY moans again, which might be mistaken for the sound of the baby.)

(Presently, MICHAEL comes out of the "mystery" suite door, #3.)

IRENE. *(looks up)* What are *you* doing up there?!

MICHAEL. Howling at the moon, what else? There's going to be a lovely moon tonight, haven't you noticed – or is that old hat to you, because *every* night there's a lovely…

IRENE. Lunatics howl at the moon.

MICHAEL. Exactly.

(**DINAH** *moans fitfully in* **IRENE**'s *room.*)

MICHAEL. *(descends stairs)* That *wasn't* me.

IRENE. I know very well who it was.

MICHAEL. Can you tell the sound of a baby's voice from a lunatic? Can you tell the sound of a woman's voice from the sound of a man's – when they cry out in their sleep?

IRENE. I think it is impossible to distinguish the age or the sex of a cry for help or a voice in pain. What were you doing in that room?

MICHAEL. Snooping. Sticking my nose where it doesn't belong. *(yawns)* Excuse me, I think I'll have a little snooze myself. (**MICHAEL** *goes into his suite and closes the door.*)

(**TOM** *sits up in bed, shakes his head, gets up, picks up his tennis raquet, pantomimes a serve, comes out on the terrace, still wrapped in his towel. The terrace is now in deep shadow, illuminated by the moon.* **IRENE** *watches* **TOM** *intently.* **TOM** *yawns, stretches, looks up to see* **IRENE.***)

TOM. Are you looking at me?

IRENE. *(flustered)* Of course not! But how could I miss you!

TOM. It's possible. It's gotten dark out here.

IRENE. I mean…dressed that way.

TOM. I'm decent, am I not? *(re: towel)* This is longer than my tennis shorts.

IRENE. *(melting, all charm)* I think you look as good in a towel as you do in a dinner jacket.

TOM. Where's Dinah?

IRENE. Lying down inside-resting.

TOM. What were you doing just now – besides looking at me?

IRENE. I thought I heard some noises down on the pier.
Fishermen, I think, bring girls there. I think they pull
up their boats after dark and use the cabanas for –
"parties." I've got to put a stop to it.

TOM. If they're not hurting anything, why not let them
have a few laughs on the rich?

IRENE. *(descends starts to terrace)* Would you like to come
down there with me now – join me in a dip? You've
already got your towel.

TOM. I don't have a bathing suit on.

IRENE. I never bother, myself.

TOM. You mean, go skinny dipping?

IRENE. *(crosses to TOM)* It's even darker down there. Your
modesty won't be compromised.

TOM. *(tactfully)* I don't think there's time. I'd better get
dressed for the party.

IRENE. There's no rush. In hot countries, Tom, we take it
slow.

TOM. *(politely)* Listen, sweetheart, you and me in the dark
in our birthday suits – I think I better sit this one out.

IRENE. *(flirtatious)* Really, Tom, the way your mind works!

(IRENE *musses* TOM*'s hair, runs her hand down the
nape of his neck as* DINAH *abruptly comes out of Irene's
bedroom onto the balcony)*

TOM. *(tactfully take* IRENE*'s hand away, "gallantly" kisses it)*
Excuse me, beautiful.

(TOM *goes to* DINAH; IRENE *"sulks."*)

(to DINAH*)* What's the matter? You have a nightmare?

DINAH. *(catching her breath)* Why, could you hear me? Was I
making sounds in my sleep?

IRENE. Like you were having an erotic dream.

(DINAH *comes down the stairs.)*

DINAH. *(to* TOM*)* Oh, honey, I was so frightened.

(TOM enfolds DINAH in his arms. There is some noise from the dock below. IRENE turns.)

IRENE. *(calling)* Who's down there? What's going on?!

DINAH. *(to TOM)* It was horrible. You were in the dream. And so was Jerry.

IRENE. *(crossing to beach stairs)* That's private property! No trespassing! Propiedad privada! No pase! *(IRENE descends to the beach, into the pit.)*

DINAH. Jerry was pushing me under some dark water – holding me down.

TOM. *(slips his arm inside her robe)* Maybe you need a little artificial respiration.

DINAH. Honnneee!

TOM. And what did you do? When Jerry held you under?

DINAH. I woke up. Where's Irene?

TOM. Gone.

(TOM kisses DINAH as MICHAEL's door opens and he comes outside in a kind of daze.)

MICHAEL. *(sees them below)* Don't...don't fight.

DINAH. Michael, what's wrong?

(MICHAEL descends the stairs. TOM and DINAH remain in an embrace.)

MICHAEL. I want the mommy and the daddy to be good to each other.

TOM. You're stoned outta your head!

DINAH. We're not fighting, darling. Don't you see? We have our arms around each other.

MICHAEL. *(to TOM, slurred)* Tell her you're sorry.

TOM. For what?

MICHAEL. For everything. And that you won't do it again. Tell her.

TOM. *(to DINAH)* I'm sorry – and I won't do it again.

MICHAEL. *(to DINAH)* Now, you tell him.

DINAH. I'm sorry, too. For everything.

MICHAEL. Now, kiss. *(They look at him.)* Go on. Please. Kiss each other.

(TOM and DINAH face each other and kiss. MICHAEL sinks to his knees before them, encircles them with his arms and buries his face against their legs.)

That's right. Love each other. Love each other.

(TOM and DINAH hold their embrace. MICHAEL gets up and goes back up to his room. CARLOS comes out of the house.)

CARLOS. Buenos tardes.

DINAH. Good evening.

TOM. Carlos.

(TOM and DINAH turn and go inside their suite as CARLOS goes about the terrace lighting some hurricane lamps.)

(DINAH and TOM sink onto their bed as the light in their suite dies out and the candle-lit glow on the terrace intensifies.)

(Some Latin music begins, as if wafting from across the water from a distance.)

(CARLOS moves to straighten the cushions on the lounges, then crosses to Ray's door. He knocks gently and enters as the music loudens.)

(IRENE comes up the stairs from the beach, passes Tom and Dinah's door. She stops, listens for a moment, then continues up to her own room, enters and closes the door.)

(MICHAEL's door opens and he steps outside, dressed in black tie. He is not drunk or drugged beyond reason, but is clearly feeling no pain. He begins to descend to the terrace as JUANITO exits the house with the empty bar cart. MICHAEL reacts. JUANITO leaves the cart, tosses his head haughtily, and goes back inside.)

(CARLOS opens the door to RAY's room and the old man exits, wearing dinner clothes. CARLOS follows, carrying a freshly ironed handkerchief which he carefully arranges

in **RAY**'s *breast pocket.* **RAY** *silently thanks him, pats him on the shoulder.* **CARLOS** *goes back into the house as* **RAY** *toddles over to the niche, takes a match and lights a votive candle before the statue.)*

MICHAEL. Good evening, sir.

*(**RAY** turns with surprise to see **MICHAEL**, gives him a little wave of the hand. **MICHAEL** bows slightly.)*

*(**RAY** weaves over to the bar, sees there is no liquor.)*

Prohibition is back.

*(**RAY** waves a hand dismissively toward **IRENE**'s room, moves toward a chair, sits down unhappily.)*

You know, Ray, you remind me of my father. He was a devout Catholic.

*(**RAY** shakes his head, wags his hand negatively.)*

Yes, you are. I can tell. My father liked a good joke and you like a good joke. And, God knows, my father liked his liquor – and the rest goes without saying. And I liked my father – and the rest goes without saying.

*(**RAY** smiles, nods appreciatively.)*

Although I was closer to my mother as a child. I thought my father a villain of sorts. But, as I got older, I grew farther away from her and closer to him – the more I grew up – became more of a man. But, unfortunately, just as we were about to finally have some respect for each other, he died.

*(**RAY**'s head drops slightly.)*

He died in my arms. And when he did, he said to me – after years of answers – or, at least, opinions – he looked up at me and said, "I don't understand any of it. I never did." *(looks up at **IRENE**'s room)* In a odd way, Irene even reminds me of my mother. Oh, she's not really like her at all - nor you like him – but you both remind me of them. Does that make any sense to you? Do you understand?

*(RAY gently beckons **MICHAEL** to come nearer. **MICHAEL** crosses to him, kneels down beside him. **RAY** wiggles his hand: " Comme si comme ça.")*

MICHAEL. *(cont.)* Oh. Yes and no. Not completely.

*(RAY smiles, puts an elbow on the arm of his chair, turns his head away, but listens as **MICHAEL** speaks – like a priest and penitent in a confessional.)*

My father was born very poor, but he made a lot of money...

(RAY nods, taps himself on the chest, knowingly.)

You, too?

(RAY does the " Comme si comme ça" bit again.)

Oh. I see. You weren't poor, but you weren't rich. Just average.

(RAY nods.)

Yes, well, my father was poor. You probably went to college, didn't you?

(RAY nods.)

Umm, well, my father didn't. But he was very smart. He was really self-educated. He read. He was bright. Especially in ways in which I am not. A whiz at arithmetic and spelling. I can't spell my name and, to me, two and two is twenty-two!

(RAY laughs.)

Anyway, he made a success of himself. Nothing like what you've done. But to me, growing up in a one-horse town, it seemed like this much. Everybody thought we were rich – and I thought so, too. That's why I identify with you – sitting here in your elegant clothes, you are how I always wanted my father to be. *(a beat)* He died. I escaped.

*(RAY pats **MICHAEL** on the head.)*

(ironically) Can I go in peace now, father?

(MICHAEL takes RAY's hand, kisses it as the doors to Irene's suite are opened by JUANITO. IRENE comes outside, regally gowned all in black, coifed, and bejeweled. She carries a handbag and a stole, trimmed in black ostrich).

IRENE. What's going on down there? What are you two talking about? Me?

MICHAEL. *(standing)* Oh, God! It's like that cliché – déjà vu all over again? You look wonderful, Irene.

IRENE. *(coquettishly)* Compliments will get you everywhere. How about a drink? And I don't mean lemonade.

MICHAEL. *(charmingly) Yes.* And Ray and I would prefer a belt to a punch – if you know what I mean.

(RAY laughs. IRENE relents, smiles, descends to the terrace.)

IRENE. I see what Dinah means. You might get to grow on one – in spite of yourself. *Carlos!*

MICHAEL. *(to RAY)* Stick with me, chum.

(RAY smiles gleefully as CARLOS appears.)

CARLOS. Si, Senora?

IRENE. *(takes key from bosom, hands it over)* Trae la bebida y heillo.

CARLOS. En sequida, Senora.

(Soft strains of a latin beat begin…)

IRENE. Oh, listen, they've started the music. And look – lanterns strung across their terrace! And candles lit in cut-out paper bags on the stone stairs. Lovely. I must remember to steal that idea sometime. *(to MICHAEL)* You and my husband seen to have become old friends.

MICHAEL. Ray and I understand each other.

(RAY nods, pats MICHAEL on the shoulder.)

IRENE. What are your plans from here – after Dinah and Tom leave?

MICHAEL. Why, to leave with them.

(**CARLOS** *returns with a tray. Several bottles of liquor and a bucket with champagne, glasses and ice. He takes them to the bar cart.* **RAY** *starts toward him.*)

IRENE. *(heading him off)* Now, now, Ray! I had this brought out for our guests.

MICHAEL. Oh, Irene! Ray's allowed one drink before dinner, you said so yourself

IRENE. Huh! He had that and more this afternoon. Isn't that right, my darling? Tell me truth, Ray. Didn't Carlos bring you a bottle this afternoon?

(**RAY** *looks away.* **IRENE** *goes to the bar cart, holds up the Scotch bottle.*)

(to **CARLOS***)* ¿Dime si le llevaste esta botella al Senor esta tarde, si o no?

CARLOS. No, Senora. No es verdad.

IRENE. ¡Mentiroso! *(to* **MICHAEL***)* He lies. He also steals wine and food and entertains women down in the cabanas. *(to* **RAY***)* How many more insults must I bear before you will dismiss this man!

(**RAY** *helplessly shakes his head.*)

(to **CARLOS***)* Go, get out! ¡Vete fuera! ¡FUERA!

(**CARLOS** *exits.*)

(to **MICHAEL***)* I'd watch him if I were you. He'll probably offer himself to you for money.

MICHAEL. If I had the money I'd pay him.

IRENE. You know by now, I don't find insolence amusing. From Carlos or from you.

MICHAEL. I think it's unfair to make accusations of Carlos. He strikes me as a man of rather admirable principles. You're fortunate that he stays.

(**RAY** *nods in agreement.*)

IRENE. Go ahead and gang up on me! See if I care.

(**RAY** *starts for the bar cart.* **IRENE** *quickly intercepts him once more.*)

IRENE. *(cont.)* Ray, you can't have any of that! The *doctor* says...

*(RAY suddenly and violently pushes her away. **MICHAEL** catches **IRENE** before she falls. **RAY** tears off the Scotch bottle cap and pours himself a substantial drink.)*

(to **MICHAEL***)* Don't let him do it! Please! Please! It's bad for his heart! *(starts to cry)* I'm not trying to be mean. I have to be strong with him. It's for his own good. Won't you help me, Michael? Please?

MICHAEL. *(puts his arm about her, comforts her)* It doesn't matter, Irene. If it makes him happy, let him have it. Because it really doesn't matter.

*(**IRENE** continues to cry as **MICHAEL** rocks her gently and **RAY** downs the drink.)*

(softly) Shhhh...quiet...don't cry. Don't cry, Mama, don't cry.

*(**IRENE** composes herself. The music across the bay changes to a Bossa Nova beat.)*

Come on, Irene, let's dance.

*(**MICHAEL** makes an attempt at moving her about the terrace.)*

IRENE. Oh, stop! I can't dance!

MICHAEL. I know you can. Can't she, Ray?

*(**RAY** laughs, nods.)*

IRENE. *(to* **RAY***)* What are you laughing at, you silly thing?! Don't try to make-up with me. I'm mad at you, Ray. Mad as can be!

*(**RAY** only laughs some more.)*

MICHAEL. Come on, now, Irene, dance with me!

IRENE. Well, we can't dance *here* – not on this pavement. I'll ruin my evening slippers. If we want to dance – we've got a dance floor. Why don't we use it? Nobody ever *does!*

MICHAEL. Where?

IRENE. *(indicating area over foyer)* Up there. It's inlaid with glazed tiles. This house was designed for parties! It was planned for living-it-up!

MICHAEL. Well, let's live-it-up! But first, how about a little drink?

IRENE. All right. I'll have one with you! Now, what do you think about that, Ray?!

MICHAEL. What'll it be – a martini?

IRENE. I never touch anything that does not come from the grape!

*(**MICHAEL** goes to the bar cart, pours himself a vodka and a glass of champagne for **IRENE**. **IRENE** has headed up to the dance floor.)*

MICHAEL. One on-the-rocks and a bit of the bubbly, literally coming up!

*(**MICHAEL** climbs the stairs. **IRENE** does a few turns about the floor. **MICHAEL** gives her the glass of champagne. They toast each other.)*

Cheers!

IRENE. Oh, I hate saying, "Cheers." I think it's so common. But, all right, "Cheers!"

*(They drink. **IRENE** catches sight of **RAY**.)*

Ray? Raaa-aaayyy?! What's the matter? Huh? Are you mad at me, my darling? Yes, you are! I can tell. Well, I'm sorry. Okay? I said, I'm sorry, Ray. Am I forgiven?

*(After a moment, **RAY** gives in and nods.)*

Oh, good! I don't want us to be upset with each other. I just want…I just want you to…*enjoy your drink!*

*(**RAY** looks at her, inscrutably. **IRENE** laughs a bit hysterically.)*

*(The door to **TOM** and **DINAH**'s room opens and they step outside. **TOM** is in black-tie. **DINAH** is resplendent in a long, simple dinner gown in a flattering warm color.)*

DINAH. Well, well, well, this sounds like a happy group!

(**IRENE** *stops laughing as* **MICHAEL** *leaves her side and goes down the steps to* **DINAH**.)

MICHAEL. Wow, do you look sensational! Gimme a kiss!

IRENE. *(ignoring* **DINAH***)* Michael! What about our dance?

MICHAEL. *(to* **DINAH***)* Some dress! Where'd you get that?

DINAH. *(kisses* **MICHAEL***'s cheek)* You'd be surprised what I can do with a needle and thread.

MICHAEL. I'll bet!

TOM. *(to* **MICHAEL***)* How do *I* look? Don't I get a kiss?

MICHAEL. You're too ugly.

IRENE. *(impatiently) Mii-chael!*

TOM. Well, Irene'll give me a kiss.

IRENE. *(to* **TOM***, petulantly)* You had your chance.

TOM. Uh-oh. I'm in the doghouse.

IRENE. No, you're not! Not tonight. Not even the *dog* is in the doghouse, Even though he's left me, too.

DINAH. *(kisses* **RAY** *on cheek)* Hello, handsome.

(**RAY** *basks in the attention.*)

TOM. *(to* **RAY***)* How're you doing, pal?

(*They shake hands warmly.* **RAY** *indicates for* **TOM** *to make drinks.*)

TOM. Champagne? Beautiful.

MICHAEL. *(to* **DINAH***)* Ray looks great this evening, don't you think? Good color.

IRENE. *(grimly, descending stairs to terrace)* It's the alcohol. It has him flushed.

DINAH. And I'd say the lady of the house looks pretty smashing.

IRENE. *(to* **TOM** *re: her dress)* Dior. Decades ago.

DINAH. And your hair – it's lovely. Did someone come in to do it?

IRENE. Juanito's been dressing my wigs ever since he's been here. You know that!

DINAH. Sometimes the really important things slip my mind.

MICHAEL. Come on, Dinah, let's dance.

> (**MICHAEL** *takes* **DINAH***'s hand and leads her up to the floor.* **RAY** *follows slowly.*)

IRENE. I thought you asked *me* to dance, Michael.

TOM. (*to* **IRENE**) We can dance. It's you and me, baby!

> (**IRENE** *gently shakes her head, moves away.* **TOM** *doesn't insist.*)

> (**MICHAEL** *and* **DINAH** *glide across the tile dance floor, dancing to the music from across the bay: Cole Porter's* You're Sensational. **MICHAEL** *sings along.**)

TOM. (*applauding*) Yeah, yeah, yeah! Couple number one! Couple number one!

> (*There is the sound of a dog barking, down by the beach.* **IRENE** *quickly crosses to the edge of the terrace.*)

MICHAEL. Was there ever – will there ever be again – anyone quite as marvelous as Cole Porter?

IRENE. Somebody's down there on the dock! I think that's Lucky barking at them! (*calling*) That's private property! – Propriedad privada!

> (*She hurries down the beach steps [into the pit].* **TOM** *looks into the darkness.* **DINAH** *and* **MICHAEL** *have stopped dancing.*)

MICHAEL. (*to* **DINAH**) What are you looking at?

DINAH. At you. What have you taken?

MICHAEL. (*simply*) A pain-killer. I had a headache. I just took something to kill the pain, Dinah.

DINAH. That's so tiresome.

MICHAEL. I know. Pretty soon it's going to be passé. Like stealing hub caps, which went out in the fifties.

> (*The telephone in the foyer rings.*)

> (**RAY** *goes toward it, looks at it helplessly.*)

---

*Please see Music Use Note on Page 3.

DINAH. It's the kids!

> (**TOM** *turns.* **DINAH** *breaks away from* **MICHAEL,** *rushes down stairs to pick up the phone.*)
>
> (*into phone*) Hello?! Si, si? Who? Qui l'appelle? Oh. Just a minute (*She puts down the receiver, comes outside.*)
> (*to* **TOM**) It's for you. It's your wife.
>
> (**TOM** *goes into the foyer to the phone.* **DINAH** *sits on a chaise.* **RAY** *goes to sit by her, takes her hand.* **DINAH** *smiles at* **RAY** *appreciatively.* **MICHAEL** *slowly descends the stairs to the terrace as the Cole Porter song ends.*)

TOM. (*into phone*) Karen? Darling?

> (**IRENE** *comes up from the beach.*)

IRENE. (*dejectedly*) There was no one. Not even Lucky – If there was anyone…they ran away. Lucky must have run away, too.

TOM. (*into phone*) Well, when do you plan to file? Well, Jesus, darling, what's the rush? (*After a moment, he hangs up, returns outside, like a sleepwalker.*)

MICHAEL. What's up, fella?

TOM. She – wants a divorce.

> (**DINAH** *gets up, goes to* **TOM.** *He doesn't respond.* **CARLOS** *enters with a tray of canapés.*)

CARLOS. Hors d'oeuvres?

IRENE. (*coolly*) Gracias. (*to group*) Come on, everybody, let's be festive!

> (**CARLOS** *serves the guests.*)

MICHAEL. (*apprehensively*) Dinah? Tom?

> (**DINAH** *turns away from* **TOM,** *who has kept his back to her, and crosses to* **MICHAEL.** **TOM** *still hasn't moved.*)

IRENE. Tom? What's wrong?

TOM. (*crosses to* **IRENE,** *turns on the charm*) Nothing, sweetheart. Nothing a little party won't cure!

IRENE. You're going to like our friends. They have a marvelous chef. The fare is strictly local. *Authentic.* I never eat French food anywhere but France. Never Italian anywhere but Italy.

TOM. You've been everywhere – done everything.

IRENE. I've never been to Hawaii.

DINAH. Neither have I. I'd like to go there – if they just wouldn't play that music.

TOM. Hawaii's great. I played a tournament there.

IRENE. You like to follow the sun, don't you?

TOM. I like to keep on the move – keep active. It keeps one from too much thinking.

IRENE. When Ray and I were first married we went around the world on our honeymoon. We went places with names that don't even exist anymore – like Ceylon. Nothing in life is very permanent, I'm afraid.

DINAH. Not even countries are forever.

IRENE. Ray bought and sold land everywhere. We lived everywhere. Now, I want to stay in one place and let the world go around me.

MICHAEL. Do you think you've achieved that – having the world revolve around you?

IRENE. In a way, yes. Ray has attained everything important for survival interest, work, ambition, accomplishment, fulfillment.

TOM. What about love?

(There's an awkward silence.)

IRENE. *(to* **CARLOS***)* Carlos, traigan el auto!

CARLOS. Si, Senora.

*(***CARLOS** *puts down the tray and goes through the foyer and off.)*

MICHAEL. I have no money and I'm nowhere. But I want to sing and dance and love and exhaust all possibilities by the time the end rolls around. So far, I'm making quiet a hash of it. I think Tom and Dinah are on the verge of a success, though.

DINAH. What makes you say that?

MICHAEL. *(clearly)* Because you both know what's essential for each other's survival. And I think you're committed to it, whether you know it or not. You may think it's not enough – but it's all you need. It's all there is. I'm sure of it.

IRENE. I wonder if, at this point in his life, Ray feels the same way.

MICHAEL. Do *you*, Irene?

(RAY reaches into his breast pocket, removes a small, elegant leather pad and a gold pencil. He writes something, pushes the pad to TOM.)

TOM. *(reads)* "There's not much between us and the grave except some personally meaningful work and an honest give-and-take relationship with, at least, one other human being."

IRENE. Oh, Ray, that's so true. So true.

(RAY turns away. IRENE covers...)

Oh, look at the time. We must be going! Just put your glasses anywhere, Juanito will straighten up. Juanito, arreglen este desastre! Let's go, children.

(DINAH's takes RAY's arm. TOM takes IRENE's. MICHAEL follows. The music from across the bay starts up again.)

Tom, *I will* dance with you, if you like! Please, dance with me at the party! I want to dance and sing and have a good time, like Michael says,...before...before the night's over.

(The group goes out through the arch to the foyer and exits the front entrance.)

(For a moment, there is silence, except for the music wafting over the water.)

(The door to IRENE's suite opens and JUANITO steps outside, wearing IRENE's high heel shoes, a feather boa, and one her wigs. He takes a lipstick and paints on a big, mocking mouth, then looks at himself in the mirror of a compact.)

JUANITO. ¡Ay, madre de Jesus!

> (**JUANITO** *descends to the terrace floor, picks up one of the full glasses of champagne and gulps it down.*)

> (**CARLOS** *comes through the foyer arch and out onto the terrace to see* **JUANITO**.)

CARLOS. *(sardonically)* Brava. Brava.

> (**JUANITO** *is momentarily chagrinned at being caught, then recovers with defiance.*)

JUANITO. *(lewdly)* Me quieres?

CARLOS. No te metas con las cosas de la Senora. Te vas arrenpentir.

> (*The door of suite #3 slowly opens and a lovely young peasant girl, steps out onto the balcony, holding a tiny baby, wrapped in a blanket.*)

JUANITO. *(looking up)* Ahhhhhh! ¡Que linda!

> (**CARLOS** *turns. The baby cries for a moment. The young mother rocks the infant in her arms as she descends the stairs.* **CARLOS** *goes up to meet her halfway. He takes the baby from her, kisses her.*)

> *(applauds)* Ah, bien. ¡Muy bien!

> (**JUANITO** *descends to* **RAY**'s *room and lets Lucky, the German Shepherd, out on a leash.*)

Ay, Lucky!

> (*The young woman and* **CARLOS**, *holding the baby, come down to the terrace. For a moment, they all seem like one big, happy family.*)

> (*The music and their laughter loudens. Suddenly, the front door in the foyer is flung open and* **IRENE**, *like a volcanic manifestation, erupts onto the terrace, screaming...*)

IRENE. Help! HELP! *HEEELLLLL-PP!!*

> (**JUANITO** *and the dog, the girl and* **CARLOS**, *holding the baby, freeze as* **TOM** *enters, carrying* **RAY** *in his arms, with* **IRENE**, **DINAH**, *and* **MICHAEL** *quickly following.*)

(There is a breathless, flash-second when all action, all sound ceases and the two groups stare at each other for an instant, like a mirrored reflection. Lucky barks, **JUANITO** *releases him, and the dog runs down the beach stairs.)*

IRENE. *(simultaneously)* What-Who? Get a doctor! ¡UN MEDICO! ¡BUSCA UN MEDICO!

*(***TOM*** carries* **RAY** *to a chaise.* **DINAH** *follows and unfastens* **RAY***'s black tie and shirt.)*

*(***CARLOS*** passes the baby to the girl and dashes to the telephone in the foyer.)*

(The girl clutches the baby and flees down the steps to the beach. **IRENE** *runs to the edge of the stage after her.)*

IRENE. Come back, you! Who are you?! ¡Para! *¡PARA!*

(The girl disappears. **IRENE** *turns on* **JUANITO***, beating him, kicking at him…)*

¡Cabrona! ¡Loca cabrona!

JUANITO. ¡No, Senora, no!

*(***CARLOS*** slams the phone down, dashes out the front door, leaving it open. Momentarily, there is the sound of a car motor pulling away.)*

*(***MICHAEL*** goes slowly toward the niche by the door to* **RAY***'s room as the phone in the foyer begins to ring.)*

IRENE. *(to* **JUANITO***)* ¡Contesta el telifono!

*(***JUANITO*** races to answer the phone.* **RAY** *revives a bit, tries to sit up.)*

MICHAEL. *(sinks to his knees)* Hail, Mary, full of grace…the Lord is with thee…

JUANITO. *(into phone)* ¿Oigo? ¿Si? Siii. Un momento.

TOM. It's all right, Ray – you just fainted.

JUANITO. *(coming outside)* Senora Dinah…telefono.

*(***DINAH*** rushes toward the foyer.* **RAY** *is making interrogative gasps…)*

TOM. We're home, Ray. We're back home.

MICHAEL. ...Pray for us sinners now and at the hour...

DINAH. (*into phone*) Hello? Yes? Yes! (*devastated*) No...no... oh, *NO!*

MICHAEL. (*murmuring*) ...Blessed art thou among women, and blessed is the Fruit of thy womb...

(**DINAH** *hangs up the phone, walks dazedly outside and into guest suite #1.* **JUANITO** *has dashed upstairs to* **IRENE**'s *room, removing the heels and wig en route.*)

...Holy Mary, mother of god...

(**TOM** *tries to restrain* **RAY** *from getting up.*)

IRENE. (*to* **RAY**) No, no, my darling, you mustn't move! Not before the doctor gets here!

(**RAY** *pushes* **IRENE** *away, tries to indicate something to* **TOM**...)

MICHAEL. ...Amen.

IRENE. (*crossing into foyer*) Oh, Tom, don't let him get up! Make him stay still! (*exiting front door*) Where can the doctor be?! Oh, why doesn't he hurry?! (*off stage*) Open the gates! Abre las rejas! Al medico!

MICHAEL. (*gets up, goes to* **RAY**) Oh, Daddy, you shouldn't be up. Please...please. You shouldn't be in the bathroom. Go back and get in your bed!

TOM. (*shaking* **MICHAEL**) Michael! What's the matter with you?

MICHAEL. (*to* **TOM**) Take care of my mother. Take her to a room down the hall – don't let her see. I'll stay with him. I'll stay with him.

TOM. Michael! Michael! (*slaps* **MICHAEL**) Dinah! Dinah! Help me!

(**TOM** *rushes to guest suite #1.*)

Dinah, help me, please!

DINAH. (*without affect*) Jerry's gotten a court order to take the kids. (*begins to break*) ...If he takes my kids from me I'll...

TOM. ...You'll die.

DINAH. ...I'll kill him! *(picks up* **TOM**'s *racquet, beats the bed)* ...I'll kill that son-of-a-bitch. I'll kill him. I'll kill that bastard, I mean it, I'll kill him! *(violently)* ...Kill him! KILL HIM!

*(***TOM*** rushes to* **DINAH**. *She collapses in his arms, sobbing.)*

*(***RAY*** makes the sign of the cross, falls backward into* **MICHAEL**'s *arms.)*

MICHAEL. Oh, Daddy...oh, my father...don't leave me. You can't be leaving me, you haven't...you haven't said it...

IRENE. *(offstage)* We need you! Help! HELP US, PLEASE!

*(***RAY*** begins to move his lips.)*

MICHAEL. Yes?...Yes?...

*(***RAY*** moves his lips and* **MICHAEL** *speaks the sentence in synchronization...)*

I...I...don't...understand...any of it. I never did.

*(***MICHAEL*** closes his arms tightly around* **RAY**. **RAY**'s *head drops backward and he dies.* **MICHAEL** *rocks him gently back and forth.)*

(The light fades out.)

(curtain)

End of Act I

ACT II

(The lights come up as daybreak would, with golden rays from the horizon [the balcony rail], continuing slowly to rise and intensify during the scene.)

(DINAH, clad in a terrycloth robe, is seated on the edge of the apron, looking out into space. MICHAEL, wearing a matching robe, comes up the steps from the beach.)

MICHAEL. What're you doing?

DINAH. Watching the luminous dawn – like in *Turandot.* What've *you* been doing? Having a swim?

MICHAEL. Just watching the pool drain. You know, we're like those plastic rafts and rings, having a last aimless float before it all runs out. Nice robe.

DINAH. Thanks. So's yours.

MICHAEL. Nice that they're in such great supply. Like a hotel in Hell.

DINAH. I wouldn't walk off with one.

MICHAEL. I wouldn't run the risk with La Reina. Are they back yet?

DINAH. Not yet.

MICHAEL. Any phone calls?

DINAH. *(stops laughing)* No. Any sign of Lucky?

MICHAEL. None. We should be so lucky as Lucky. And no sign of Carlos and the girl. They all must have all gotten out while the getting was good. *About this night!*

DINAH. I'm going to be like Tom – close my eyes and hope it all goes away.

MICHAEL. It won't. There's no way out. I've tried all the exits. Except suicide. But, of course, that takes guts.

DINAH. *(distressed at the thought)* Please, Michael, I've got such a headache.

51

MICHAEL. Take a pill. Take *two* pills: one for the headache and one to get high.

DINAH. I take it you've already taken your own advice?

MICHAEL. I don't pop anything serious.

DINAH. It's *all* serious. You were a mess last night.

MICHAEL. It's the weird grass I bought here. I've never been so spaced in my life. Grass is mostly my scene at the moment. *Good* grass. Viet Green, Panama Red, Acapulco Gold. I light up just like a traffic signal. Why didn't you drive in town with them?

DINAH. Coroners are *not* my favorite. No, that's not why I couldn't make it. For the first time in my life I just couldn't *do* something. I told them I wanted to stay in case the lawyer in New York called. But the truth is, Michael, I've run down. Down and out. And I'm... frightened. Why didn't *you* go?

MICHAEL. Irene didn't ask me. Frightened? *You?*

DINAH. Yeah, me. I can't think of anything but that rich kids' prison in the Alps that Jerry's taken the boys to.

MICHAEL. He going to put them in boarding school?! Didn't your lawyer have any suggestions?

DINAH. Just one.

MICHAEL. That Tom marry you.

DINAH. I wouldn't ask him to do such a thing. Never. Ever.

MICHAEL. What other cheery news did the lawyer have?

DINAH. I've been served with papers labeling me an unfit mother – living in sin in front of the children.

MICHAEL. "Living in sin." That *would* be grounds for damnation.

DINAH. *And* exposing them to a degenerate.

MICHAEL. *That* would be me.

DINAH. Just when you baby sit.

MICHAEL. Jerry knows I baby sit?

DINAH. He hired a private detective. He knew every time I went out with Tom and left them in a hotel with you.

MICHAEL. Did it ever occur to you that Jerry's an ex-chorus boy? I know there are *straight* chorus boys, just like there're straight hair dressers and decorators and florists. Be that as it may...

DINAH. Jerry's not gay. Although he *was* always plagued with itching asshole. But I'm sure that was something else.

MICHAEL. I'm sure. Gays are far less butt-centric, if you will, than most people think. What'd he do for it, or don't you know? The itching asshole, I mean.

DINAH. Well, I know he tried every salve or lotion or talcum known to man. He even put athlete's foot powder on it. I don't recommend that.

MICHAEL. Jerry *is* The Itching Asshole! Thank God, the kids take after you. Jerry's such a wimp – what the English call "wet" – he's soooo wet. But you...*you've* got guts.

DINAH. *(drily)* You mean you think I have the courage to kill myself?

MICHAEL. That's not what I mean at all, and you know it.

DINAH. I'm not so strong. Honestly. I told you I was frightened. I haven't done so much for a little girl from Van Nuys, California.

MICHAEL. I'd say Boston, Beacon Hill or Philly. Went to...

DINAH. Farmington. I know that's what you'd say.

MICHAEL. Or Smith or Stephens.

DINAH. I'd say Santa Monica Junior College – and it's a wonder I made *that* for one semester.

MICHAEL. Flunk out?

DINAH. No. I won a beauty contest. And Jerry saw the photographs.

MICHAEL. And overnight it was searchlights in the sky and Twentieth Century-Fox presents...

(He lies back, waves his arms in a crisscross fashion, intones [badly] the famous fanfare.)

DINAH. Hardly. But Monroe and I *were* signed on the same day and given our names. She was M.M. and I was D.D. and I don't have to tell you how things alliteratively worked-out.

MICHAEL. I thought you were fabulous. Freckles and all.

DINAH. She got the bugle beads, I got the slacks and trench coats.

MICHAEL. I thought you were so chic and classy!

DINAH. Well, I never sat on cakes of ice on the fourth of July or jumped through paper hearts on Valentine's Day.

MICHAEL. You were sort of a man-woman symbol. Blurred the edges.

DINAH. Vaguely dykey, is what you're trying to say.

MICHAEL. Well, all the great ones were. And some of them not so vaguely.

DINAH. Sweetie, it takes a long time to find out what your style is, and when you find it, stick to it.

MICHAEL. You know, Dinah, if there were ever any chance of my…well, it could only be someone like you.

DINAH. Like me, or like that Hollywood image you have of me?

MICHAEL. Like I think you really are. You're real to the sprocket, Maude.

DINAH. You mean I'm a pal.

MICHAEL. Yeah. Why can't a gal be more like a pal? I wish I could have met you when you could have shown me the ropes. I love you, Dinah. I really do.

DINAH. Shut up and tell me why you think I didn't make it big in pictures.

(*There is a door slam.* TOM, IRENE *and* JUANITO *have come in the front entrance.* IRENE *stops to speak to* JUANITO *in the foyer as* TOM *comes out onto the terrace. The sun is higher and brighter with less color.*)

IRENE. Haz cafe.

JUANITO. Si, Senora. (**JUANITO** *exits from the foyer to the kitchen.*)

TOM. *(to* **DINAH***)* Have you heard anymore?

DINAH. *(shakes her head)* I want to meet with the lawyers in person. I made a reservation on the noon plane to New York.

TOM. For how many?

DINAH. Only myself. I didn't know if you'd want to come – or if you and Michael would be going on someplace else.

IRENE. *(comes outside)* – You're leaving?

DINAH. I have to, Irene.

IRENE. Just when I need you most.

DINAH. I'm sorry, but my children need me too. What arrangements have you made?

TOM. Jesus, you wouldn't believe the red tape!

IRENE. Cremation. But there are so many papers and legalities to be dealt with before I can...Tom has been a great help. I couldn't have managed without him. Won't you please stay just a little while longer? We can all go back to New York together.

DINAH. I can't wait.

IRENE. Tom?

TOM. I...have to go with Dinah.

DINAH. You don't have to.

(**TOM** *goes to the bar, pours himself a straight Scotch.*)

IRENE. *(to* **TOM***)* Awfully early, isn't it? Juanito's making some coffee.

TOM. I'm a big boy, Irene. I can take care of myself.

IRENE. Really? And what about you, Michael? Will you stay and help me?

MICHAEL. Well...if Tom doesn't go with Dinah – I suppose I'll move on with him.

IRENE. But if they *do* go together, stay here. Stay here with *me*.

MICHAEL. Well, I…

IRENE. *(crosses to* MICHAEL*)* You won't have to worry about anything. Your company will be all that is required, and it will be such a consolation. You can simply live here and be taken care of. You can rest – and write.

*(*JUANITO *enters with a tray of coffee and rolls, puts it down on the dining table.)*

MICHAEL. It's a very gracious offer.

IRENE. Think about it. Coffee, Dinah?

DINAH. Thanks, no.

IRENE. *(to* JUANITO*)* Where is the silver service? Why have you brought these horrid plastic things? These are the kitchen dishes. These are what the help use!

MICHAEL. I believe it's up top.

IRENE. What? What's up where?

*(*JUANITO *sheepishly starts toward the foyer.)*

MICHAEL. Your silver service. *(points to guest suite #3)* It's up there.

TOM. What are you talking about, Swifty?

IRENE. Juanito! Ven aqui!

JUANITO. *(stops)* Si, Senora.

IRENE. *(to* MICHAEL*)* Explain yourself.

MICHAEL. *(after a beat)* After I heard the crying, I traced it up to the guest suite on top. And there was the baby. And Carlos and the girl – packing silver into some rather elegant suitcases. And canned goods and booze. They looked up at me, but said nothing, and neither did I, and I left. I went back up a while ago. The luggage is still there and so is all the stuff in it. I guess the family got out on shorter notice than expected. If you want your silver coffee pot, Irene, it's in Ray's Louis Vuitton in the upper guest quarters. I know it was Ray's because his initials were stenciled on it.

IRENE. *(calmly)* Juanito, donde esta la cafetera de plata?

JUANITO. *(shakes his head)* No se, Senora.

> *(IRENE turns and crosses to the stairs. JUANITO follows.)*
>
> *(panicking)* No, no, Senora! La culpa es de Carlos!
>
> *(A heated altercation ensues, ad-libbed Spanish between JUANITO and IRENE as she leads the way up the stairs, and enters guest suite #3. Meanwhile...)*

DINAH. *(crossing to MICHAEL)* Michael, don't stay! Whatever you do – even if you just keep running, *keep running* – but don't stay here.

MICHAEL. Can I come with you?

DINAH. It's time for you to be on your own. But you must *get out.*

TOM. Dinah's right. If you stay here – it'll be the end of you.

MICHAEL. *(to TOM)* What are *you* going to do? Go with Dinah – or move on to somewhere new?

TOM. *(turns away)* I don't know. I just don't know.

> *(IRENE appears on the balcony outside suite #3 with the silver coffee pot in her hand.)*

IRENE. *(calmly)* Well, well, well. Michael, you'd be invaluable to have around. *(descending stairs)* Juanito blames Carlos. It was just as I suspected all along. That animal was taking this poor boy's hard-earned money in exchange for – an occasional favor. And to keep Juanito quiet, he was blackmailing him into harboring his pregnant slut who had his whining bastard in that very room. How do you like that?!

TOM. Fantastic.

IRENE. I'll say it's fantastic. It's *something!* Juanito tells me, Michael, that Carlos offered himself to you down on the beach. Did you find Carlos attractive?

MICHAEL. Yes. In a venereal sort of way.

IRENE. Juanito was quite jealous.

MICHAEL. Carlos had several things for sale. But the only thing I bought and paid for was a lid of local grass. I couldn't afford both it *and* Carlos, and I figure you have to be realistic and make up your mind what's most important to you. Priorities. It's something I've picked up from Dinah.

DINAH. That's my boy.

MICHAEL. Juanito has nothing to be jealous about. All that was blown was my fifty bucks. The really odd thing happened when I was smoking the dope on the beach. I found some fresh footprints, but there was no one around. I followed the tracks but they began to fade and were washed away. So I ran back to the spot where I'd first seen them and discovered a set of *new* tracks. I couldn't tell whether the same person had returned, as I had done, or whether a third party had passed by. But there was no one around and suddenly I thought, timing *is* everything.

IRENE. Is that all? So what?

MICHAEL. And so I masturbated into the footprints.

IRENE. *(after a moment)* I'll tell you as I have always told those who work for me – when you want things which you cannot afford, I will take care of such arrangements. If you stayed, Michael...

MICHAEL. I said I'll think about it.

IRENE. Very well. Did Lucky ever come back?

MICHAEL. Eh...no.

IRENE. Oh, well. I think I'll try to rest now. *(with an edge)* Dinah, I don't suppose you'd leave without saying goodbye.

DINAH. *(slightly stung)* I wouldn't dream of it, Irene. Surely you know that.

> (**IRENE** *goes up the steps to her suite in the private tower.* **JUANITO** *follows, carrying the silver coffee pot.)*

IRENE. I don't know anything anymore. I merely want to avoid any further disappointment. Knock on my door even if I'm asleep. You know, that son-of-a-bitch Carlos probably stole Lucky too.

(IRENE enters her room. JUANITO follows her and closes the door.)

DINAH. That woman has a Ph.D. in Guilt. *(DINAH begins to move.)*

TOM. Where're you going?

DINAH. To get my clothes and get a taxi.

TOM. I'll – change the reservation. Make it for two.

DINAH. That's up to you.

TOM. Don't you *want* me to come with you?

DINAH. Oh, Tom, what I want is beside the point. The choice is yours.

(She goes into suite #1. TOM goes to the bar.)

MICHAEL. Awfully early for that, Tom. Juanito's made some coffee.

TOM. *(takes drink)* Screw you and the boat that brought you over!

MICHAEL. It was a plane this time, remember? *(MICHAEL goes to pour some coffee.)* Well, I'm gonna have some coffee in a plastic cup. What *will* the neighbors think?

TOM. What is it with me and women? Huh, Swifty? Can you tell me?

MICHAEL. Sorry, I'm gonna slither out of that one. How was it in town?

TOM. The laughs were *not* at the creamatorium.

MICHAEL. Well, it was fast.

TOM. It was a slow day. They were glad to see us.

MICHAEL. *(puts on dark glasses)* Wow, that sun is getting hot!

TOM. Yeah, the heat's really on!

MICHAEL. By noon, it's going to be a blazing, blistering, unbreathable inferno. To Hell with tonight, there's going to be a hot time in the ol' town by *noon!*

TOM. You wanna drink? Or are you half-in-the-bag already?

MICHAEL. I'm not anything. I'm not high, I'm not low, I'm nothing. Nada. Niente. Nicht. In spades.

TOM. *(finishes his drink, pours another)* Come on, Swifty, have a silver bullet.

MICHAEL. No.

TOM. Well, that's a switch.

MICHAEL. Are you trying to *force* alcohol upon me?!

TOM. Don't get raggy with *me!*

MICHAEL. You're the one who's on the rag! What's with you? Belting 'em down like there's no tomorrow and it's not even high, hot noon!

TOM. *(grimly)* I'm in a bind, man. I'm in one helluva spot.

MICHAEL. Umm. Actually, you're *on* the spot.

TOM. *(takes a drink)* You better believe it. If I marry her – which is what I've got to do to get her off the hook, to save her kids for her – then I'm screwed. I'm stuck. My life's – well, not my own anymore.

MICHAEL. You wouldn't mind being "stuck" with Karen, would you?

TOM. On the other hand, if I walk – say, "bye-bye, thanks for shaping me up and the waltz around the park" – then I'm nailed for what I've done: let her down. Carry around that monkey on my back for whatever happens to her.

MICHAEL. And what do you think's going to happen to her?

TOM. She'll lose the kids and crack – split right down the middle – spin out in space for good. She's already seeing a psychiatrist. Did you know that?

MICHAEL. So? It wouldn't do *you* any harm.

TOM. A lot of good it's done *you.*

MICHAEL. It might have. I pissed all over it – stop, start, show, no show, show-up late, show-up late and drunk. That's no way to run a war.

TOM. Why don't you go back? Start over.

MICHAEL. Dinah says the same thing. Karen even offered to pay for it if I would go. I wonder what Irene would do? I know what Irene would do: pay the two dollars.

TOM. Your mothers. Did you ever get far enough for the doctor to point that out to you?

MICHAEL. They're *your* mothers too. You and I have a lot of the same hang-ups – except mine are gay and yours are straight. It's no coincidence that we are friends. It's not a big accident that with the females in our lives I do their hair and you marry them.

TOM. Why don't you have a drink?

MICHAEL. Because, goddamit, I don't want one!

TOM. Now, now, take it easy.

MICHAEL. I'm already shaking my guts out, and I want to try to make one lucid decision. If you can believe it – I'm trying to sober up.

TOM. Well, I'm trying to get drunk.

MICHAEL. That much seems obvious.

TOM. Swifty?

MICHAEL. What?

TOM. What am I going to do?

MICHAEL. Whatever it is you *have* to do. To keep your…for lack of a better word…integrity. To keep your sanity. You've been brought up to do the right thing. You could never do anything less.

TOM. And what's that?

MICHAEL. I can't live your life for you, Tom – make your decisions for you. Dinah can't. Karen couldn't. For once you're going to have to do it yourself *for* yourself all *by* yourself And when you do, you have no idea the relief you'll feel.

TOM. You dirty, cocksucking bastard.

MICHAEL. Now, now, take it easy.

TOM. Swifty?

MICHAEL. What?

TOM. You know what?

MICHAEL. You're gonna tell me how much you love me.

TOM. You son-of-a-bitch.

MICHAEL. You've called me worse names. And in the recent past, I might add.

TOM. You know I don't mean it. You know I *do* love you.

MICHAEL. Yeah, I know. I'll have a pitcher of stingers and a box of Kleenex, please.

TOM. *(enthusiastic about* **MICHAEL**'s *drinking)* Good!

MICHAEL. No, Tom, I'm kidding. I know it's hard to believe, but I really don't want a drink. I want to try and stop. What you said just now is a high in itself.

(The front bell is rung by hand.)

TOM. What's that?

MICHAEL. The gate bell out front, I think.

(It rings again. **TOM** *goes to the bar to replenish his drink.* **MICHAEL** *goes into the foyer to open the front entrance.* **TOM** *downs his drink and follows.)*

*(***JUANITO** *comes out of* **IRENE**'s *door and goes up to guest suite #3. Momentarily, he returns with a large Louis Vuitton suitcase. He surreptitiously comes down the stairs, but quickly has to take refuge in* **MICHAEL**'s *suite #2, as* **MICHAEL** *returns with Ray's ashes, wrapped in a box from a crematorium.)*

TOM. *(re: box of ashes)* Where're you going to put them?

MICHAEL. I'll leave that up to Irene. Meanwhile, how about over here beneath the statue. *(***MICHAEL** *crosses to place the box in the niche below the statue of the Virgin Mary.)*

TOM. That's good. Christ, can you believe this is how we're all gonna end up?

MICHAEL. Air mailed to New York? We make the mistake of thinking that "if we could just get away from it all, everything would be okay." But it never is.

TOM. You mean trying to escape with booze and pills.

MICHAEL. And sex and religion and time and space. *(re: box of ashes)* This is the only escape.

TOM. I just shut off my brain, no matter where I am.

MICHAEL. It's the same thing. We all seek some refuge right down the line, from the day we come into the world. As if we want to go back into the womb. Maybe we just don't want to be born in the first place.

TOM. Stop it, Swifty.

MICHAEL. Too "down" for you?

TOM. *I* want to live. I don't want to go backwards, keep doing the same things over and over.

MICHAEL. Is that why you drink your breakfast?

TOM. I'm just *afraid* of going forward. What if I can't cut it? It's safer being a kid all one's life. Look at you.

MICHAEL. Yeah, I'm the poster boy for arrested development.

TOM. What if I can't make it as a adult? As a man?

(They look at each other for a moment. **TOM** *picks up his glass and the bottle of Scotch, crosses to guest suite #1 and enters.* **MICHAEL** *goes to the niche, kneels down to pray.)*

(The door to guest suite #2 opens and **JUANITO** *struggles down the stair with Ray's Vuitton case and Michael's Olivetti typewriter.)*

*(***JUANITO** *sees the box of Ray's ashes in the niche, lets out a little cry, drops the cases and makes the sign of the cross.)*

MICHAEL. Going somewhere? Marbella? Madrid? Maybe just to Hell in a Vuitton handbag with the rest of us.

*(***MICHAEL** *crosses to* **JUANITO**. *A moment later and they engage in a fierce struggle. There are muffled screams, ad libs in Spanish, some garments are torn, and above all, the jangling sound of Juanita's gold jewelry.)*

*(***JUANITO** *eventually triumphs over* **MICHAEL**, *hurls him aside.* **JUANITO** *hastens to pick up Ray's Vuitton*

case. It is all he can manage. **MICHAEL** *gets to his feet and chases him offstage right.)*

(MICHAEL stops, gets his breath, picks up his Olivetti and painfully climbs the stairs to his door, guest suite #2.)

(After a moment, IRENE comes out of her bedroom, rubbing her eyes, having had a fitful nap. The light comes up in Tom and Dinah's room on the ground floor, guest suite #1. He's sitting on the bed, drinking. DINAH is now dressed in a pants suit and is finishing her packing, about to close her luggage.)

(IRENE descends to the terrace, sees the box with RAY's ashes in the niche.)

IRENE. *(panicked)* Dinah! DINAH!

(DINAH rushes outside. IRENE is weaving, as if she's about to faint. DINAH's helps her to a chaise longue. IRENE clings to DINAH's hand.)

IRENE. *(indicating the niche)* Look. Look. I *can't* look.

DINAH. *(glances at niche)* Yes. Tom told me. Did you get any sleep?

IRENE. *(gasps)* Such as it was. Such horrible nightmares. *(fans the air)* Such heat and humidity.

DINAH. Yes, I can hardly get my breath too.

IRENE. You're not really serious about going.

DINAH. Yes, Irene. I'm dead earnest.

IRENE. But you can't be!

DINAH. I've called the Hilton. The concierge is sending a car.

IRENE. *(Standing)* No! You can't go!

DINAH. I *have* to go. I'm sorry, but it's what I have to do.

IRENE. I said you can't go off and leave me like this!

DINAH. Irene, don't...don't misunderstand. It's not my intention to abandon you, it's what I must do. Don't make it difficult for both of us.

IRENE. I understand. And I *want* to make it difficult!

DINAH. Honestly, Irene, there's nothing more to say.

(**DINAH** *turns, starts away.* **IRENE** *dashes after her, blocks her.*)

IRENE. *(desperately)* Dinah, Tom doesn't love you. He'll leave you. Stay with me and I'll take care of Jerry. My lawyers will handle everything. Tell Tom to leave without you. Tell him you don't need him.

DINAH. *(coolly)* Excuse me.

IRENE. *(lashes out)* All right! Go on and chase after him. Rope him, tie him to you, drag him with you across the world.

(**DINAH** *stops, stunned by the barrage. Inside suite #1,* **TOM** *listens silently.*)

(relentlessly) You can't make him love you if he doesn't. You may make him marry you but you can't make him love you because he loves his ex-wife. And he always will, even if you never let him out of your sight. You'll always know, he doesn't love you.

DINAH. Aren't you talking about yourself, Irene?

IRENE. What do you mean?!

DINAH. I mean you're talking about you and what you've done with your life, and the man in your life. You're not talking about *me* – not about *Tom.*

IRENE. Oh, yes, I am!

DINAH. Oh, no, no, no, dear lady. You're talking about yourself and I'm not like you. If I were ever headed in that direction, I hope I've found out in time. I hope I'll never let myself be like you.

IRENE. Like me? Like what?

DINAH. Bitter and barren.

IRENE. That's not the truth!

DINAH. You've built this house in the hot sun and it is as cold as an icecap. You've reduced your friends to neuter toys, hired one servant who's was no threat and got rid of the one who was. You made a eunuch of your husband.

IRENE. You don't know anything about me! Everything I ever got in life was because I was shrewd and strong. Ray was a smart man but he never would have achieved what he did if it hadn't been for me. And if I got bitter along the way it was because I got tired. I was never a part of anything in my life. I was never just naturally included. I was never attractive and wanted for myself I had to force my way, *all* the way. You don't know anything about that. And you don't know anything about *me.*

DINAH. *(turns)* I must...get out of here.

IRENE. *(warningly)* You're going to lose. You're going to lose your Tom, you're going to lose your children, you're going to lose your mind!

(**DINAH** *goes inside guest suite #1.* **TOM** *stands. They silently stare at each other. She goes to close her luggage.)*

IRENE. *(stumbling about)* Michael? – Michael – *MIIICHAELLL!!!*

TOM. *(to* DINAH*)* Wait!

DINAH. I'm through waiting for nothing. Through hanging around.

TOM. *(indecisively)* I mean...I don't know what I mean, but...wait!

DINAH. You don't want me to go. You don't want to go *with* me. Tom, what *do* you want?

TOM. *(ruthlessly)* I don't want you to *change* things!

DINAH. *(realizes)* You're drunk! And you only get down to business when you're blotto. It's bye-bye to the charmer. The polite little rich boy with all the manners tucks his tail and the real you shows his face.

TOM. *(irrationally)* You're forcing me to make a decision!

(**DINAH** *picks up her bags,* **TOM** *rushes to snatch them from her, hurls them across the room.)*

TOM. *WAIT!* Things'll be the same! For a minute they will be!

DINAH. If I just stand here in one spot, not move, not breathe, nothing will change! Is that it?

TOM. For a minute, no.

DINAH. Have you taken leave of your senses? Or just reverted to childhood? You're like the kids when I wake them in the morning to go to school. All I hear is give me five more minutes – one more minute – anything, anything to put off, postpone, avoid the unavoidable – having to face the world, face life!

TOM. You think you know me pretty well. You pick up a guy in a strange town…

DINAH. It wasn't strange to me, I lived there. You were the foreigner. The stranger. And I didn't pick you up – I picked-up with you.

TOM. You picked me up off the ground, Dinah. I was flat.

DINAH. Yeah, I did. And don't you forget it.

TOM. You gave me a place to live…

DINAH. You weren't exactly out on the street. A suite at the Connaught is hardly what one would call "roughing it."

TOM. Believe me, it was rough. Until you gave me a place… at your table…in your house…in your bed.

DINAH. I gave you nothing but a hard time.

TOM. You figured out what my next move was.

DINAH. I boiled you an egg. I made you shave. I pressed your pants.

TOM. You pressed my brain. You changed my life.

DINAH. What was I thinking of? Myself, I guess. I was lonely. I fell in love.

TOM. And now, you think you know me. Know my traits – hide from reality – keep my head under a rock.

(**DINAH** *is silent.*)

Dinah, talk to me.

DINAH. Why can't you talk unless you're drunk?

TOM. The booze helps me.

DINAH. No wonder you drove Karen nuts.

TOM. Who's drunk – me or you?

DINAH. I'm *not.*

TOM. Then I'm the one who's suppose to be hostile.

DINAH. That never made it all right.

TOM. I know.

DINAH. How did Karen stand it?

TOM. She couldn't.

DINAH. Silence. Denial. A fight. And the next day…

TOM. Flowers.

DINAH. And never any mention of the night before. All very proper. All very well brought up. All very un-real.

TOM. I wonder if Karen will marry that guy she's going with? I wonder if they talk to each other? I wonder if they'll live in our house?

DINAH. You were two kids *playing* house. *Playing* married. *Playing* grownup!

TOM. *S*he was growing up. She was trying. I wouldn't let her. She wanted us to get help, but in my family, if you saw a psychiatrist, it meant you were…it was something shameful.

(**TOM** *dissolves into tears.* **DINAH** *goes to him, tries to hold him in her arms.*)

DINAH. Tom…Tommy…darling…don't…don't…

TOM. *(pushes her, harshly)* Get away from me! Don't come around smothering me with your goddamn understanding! Mothering me like Irene did Ray, like you do Michael! Mother your kids, but lay off me! You may think I'm a child, but I'm not!

DINAH. *(letting him have it)* Then act like it, goddamit! Grow-up and act like it!

TOM. Stop making me feel guilty for something I'm not guilty off. Why the fuck should I be responsible for you?!

DINAH. You're drunk! Drunk and crazy!

TOM. You've made me that way! You've put me in the middle and locked me in!

DINAH. Nobody's holding you! Tom, for Christ's sake – for your own sake take a look at yourself

TOM. I'm afraid.

DINAH. Of what?

TOM. I don't want to talk about it now.

DINAH. Talk about it! For once, *talk!* Afraid of what – giving up this golden boy image you have of yourself?

TOM. Isn't that really why you were attracted to me? Isn't that about all the...all the...power I have? Isn't that all there is to me?

DINAH. You can't believe that. You *are* attractive. That's a very real part of you – but only a part. You can't believe that's all I see in you.

TOM. I think maybe now you only want to...use me.

DINAH. To get the children back?

TOM. Well?

DINAH. I think we'd better clear the air on that score right this minute. Let me tell you here and now I want to let you off the hook – if you think you're *on* the hook. I couldn't live with that. I don't want anything from you that you don't want to give.

TOM. And right here and now, I want to tell you that if it hadn't been for meeting you in London when I did, I *would* be locked-up somewhere for real. Or dead. I know I thought about killing myself. Who knows whether I would or not if it weren't for you.

(**DINAH** *goes to collect her two bags which have been scattered across the room.*)

If we were to get married...would you think I was doing it because I love you, or would you think I was doing it out of my guilt over a sense of responsibility toward you?

DINAH. If I were to get married...would you think I was doing it because I love you, or would you think I was doing it simply to hang on to my kids?

TOM. I know which one I feel you'd be doing.

DINAH. I know which one I feel you'd be doing.

TOM. I don't think it's the one you think I think it is.

DINAH. Well, I certainly hope it's not the one you think I think it is.

*(Silence between them. **DINAH** exits the room with her bags. **TOM** goes into the bath and closes the door.)*

*(The terrace is empty. **DINAH** puts down her cases, shields her eyes from the sun. Tears pour forth, and she sits on a piece of luggage and cries.)*

*(**MICHAEL** exits his suite, showered and changed, but still noticeably weak. He catches sight of **DINAH**…)*

MICHAEL. Dinah, if you've got to have a nervous breakdown, the Costa Schmosta, out-of-season, is not the place to do it.

DINAH. *(straightens, wipes eyes, digs in bag)* It's just so fucking bright I can't even see to find my sun glasses.

*(**IRENE** comes up the beach steps.)*

IRENE. *(to **MICHAEL**)* There you are. I've been calling. Where were you?

MICHAEL. *(descending to terrace)* I've been in a daze. But now, I think I've finally come to.

*(**TOM** exits the bath in guest suite #1, carrying his valise. He continues onto the terrace, stops, looks at the group…)*

Tom, are you going to marry Dinah?

TOM. *(firmly)* Yes.

IRENE. Do you love her?

TOM. Irene, if you tried to make it on that alone, the whole thing would be over before you'd get the wedding presents unwrapped.

IRENE. What'll hold you together – guilt?

TOM. Decisions. Who can make them and who can stick to them. And money. Who's got it and who needs it – who can pay the bills. And, of course, kids. Those goddamn little beasts. The only thing worse than having them is not having them. All of that holds you together. That's the real stuff, that's what makes you know what the word *"responsible"* means. Being responsible – for yourself, for others – that spells survival. And you have to hang on to survive. To hang on to each other. If that's not love, I don't know what it is. Does that answer your question?

DINAH. You forgot your tennis racquet.

(There is an offstage car horn, followed by the gate bell.)

TOM. *(to* **DINAH***)* Would you get it for me? I'll take care of the bags and meet you at the gate.

*(***DINAH** *nods sweetly, hurries back inside guest suite #1.)*

So long, Swifty.

MICHAEL. G'bye, gorgeous.

*(***TOM** *and* **MICHAEL** *hug each other.* **TOM** *picks up his and* **DINAH***'s luggage.)*

TOM. Thank you, Irene. You have my most sincere sympathy. *(He exits through the foyer out the front entrance.)*

*(***DINAH** *comes out of suite #1 with* **TOM***'s racquet.)*

DINAH. I'll write to you, Irene. And please believe me, when I say I feel truly and deeply saddened. *(She moves to* **MICHAEL***.)* Keep cool, kid. And keep *moving!*

*(***MICHAEL** *smiles.* **DINAH** *exits out the front entrance.* **MICHAEL** *turns to go upstairs.)*

IRENE. *(apprehensively)* Where are you going?

MICHAEL. To get my things and get on my way.

IRENE. Not you too.

MICHAEL. I know it's what I must do.

IRENE. You all can't desert me here with just servants and a dead man!

MICHAEL. The servants have left too.

*(***MICHAEL** *starts up toward guest suite #2.* **IRENE** *charges after him, grabs his arm.)*

IRENE. What are you saying? Where's Juanito?

MICHAEL. Stole you out of house and home and hit the high road.

IRENE. You're lying!

MICHAEL. Call him and see if he comes. All that remains are the remains of your husband.

(MICHAEL *continues up to suite #2.* IRENE *rushes about.*)

IRENE. *(calling)* Juanito! Vuelvan! Juan, come back! VUELVAN! VUELVAN! There *is* no one here! There's no one left! *(She rushes to the niche, picks up the box with* RAY*'s ashes, clutches them to her.)*

(MICHAEL *exits suite #2, carrying his bag. He descends to the terrace as* IRENE *goes to him.*)

Michael! Don't go! Please!

MICHAEL. Irene, you would suffocate me and, eventually, I'd finish you.

IRENE. We'd be friends!

MICHAEL. We'd be perfect victims for each other. You'd make me into another Ray and I'd make you into another mother – just as I've done with so many women before you.

IRENE. We'd be different!

MICHAEL. We'd destroy each other so neatly, so sweetly – it almost seems unthinkable not to proceed.

IRENE. What am I going to do?

MICHAEL. Let go, Irene. Let Ray rest in the Mediterranean. Where he retired to, where he was happy for a while.

IRENE. I only did what I thought was best for him. I only did what I thought was right.

MICHAEL. Perhaps. But now it's time to think what's best for yourself.

(IRENE *looks over* MICHAEL*'s shoulder, screams.*)

IRENE. No! – Go away! Michael, help me! *Vayanse!* He dicho *vayanse! VAYANSE!*

(CARLOS comes up the beach steps, followed by the young peasant girl, carrying the baby, wrapped in a blanket. CARLOS has Lucky, the German shepherd, on a leash.)

(The light is now brighter, whiter and higher and more colorless than ever.)

CARLOS. I came back to pay my respects to the Senor. I heard that he has died.

IRENE. You stole our motor boat!

CARLOS. When we left last night – with our child – we took the boat, yes, but we have returned it.

IRENE. You were harboring this woman and child behind my back, hoarding food and liquor. Planning to steal my silver – you've come back for those things! I'm going to call the police!

CARLOS. *(calmly)* No, Senora, that is not the truth.

MICHAEL. It doesn't matter anyway. They've already been stolen. If you're going to report a theft, Irene, Juanito is the culprit, not this man.

IRENE. *(to CARLOS)* You hate me! You always have! You've come back to harm me!

CARLOS. We have come back to see if we can help you.

IRENE. You want something! You want money!

CARLOS. If you wish my services – then I will work for you. For money, yes. I consider the exchange a fair one. I looked after the Senor's needs and he gave me money. Extra money. He wanted me to bring my family here. He wanted me to have his fine things – his luggage and tea set. He said it belonged to his mother. He wanted me to take his suitcases because he knew he was never going to use them again. He told me to take the food and liquor. I stole nothing.

IRENE. You lie!

CARLOS. I tell the truth.

MICHAEL. In the end, it's simply easier to tell the truth. I must go now. Thank you for your hospitality. Will you...kiss me good-bye?

(IRENE doesn't move. MICHAEL picks up his bags and crosses to her, kisses her on each cheek.)

MICHAEL. *(cont.)* Adios, Senora.

IRENE. *(quietly)* Adios, Senor.

(MICHAEL exits through the front entrance. IRENE turns to CARLOS as the light intensifies.)

IRENE. Your wife…can take…your child…up to your room.

CARLOS. *(to GIRL)* Sube la criatura – nosotros nos quedamos.

(CARLOS gives the GIRL the leash. She moves quickly up the stairs to guest suite #3 and goes inside with the baby and the animal.)

(IRENE looks at CARLOS, raises the box of Ray's ashes slightly…)

IRENE. At sunset. When it's cool. We'll use the motorboat.

(CARLOS nods. After a moment, he crosses to IRENE and puts his arms around her. IRENE gently rests her head against his chest.)

(The baby cries offstage.)

(The predominant source light is now directly overhead, as if the sun is at the highest and hottest time of the day…)

(blackout)

End of Act II

The End

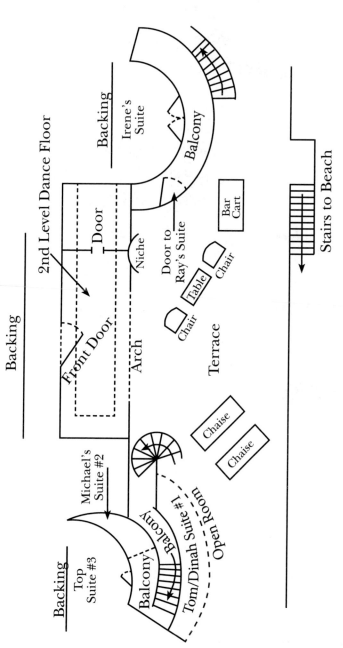

Remote Asylum

Also by
Mart Crowley...

Avec Schmaltz

The Boys in the Band

A Breeze From the Gulf

For Reasons that Remain Unclear

The Men from the Boys

Please visit our website **samuelfrench.com** for complete descriptions and licensing information.

OTHER TITLES AVAILABLE FROM SAMUEL FRENCH

AVEC SCHMALTZ

Mart Crowley

Comedy / 4m, 3f

This two-act comedic collision seems, at first, like a straightforward romp about marital grumblings. But there are all sorts of surprising complexities in the failed marriage of Kit, the WASP flame-haired rich girl, and Manny, the wry, wise-cracking Jewish TV composer which has produced two precocious, sassy children and a situation in which the ex-wife and the ex-husband can't seem to live with each other or without each other. "Avec Schmaltz" (a phrase European musicians would ironically use to instruct violinists how to emotion-ally heat-up their romantic string passages) is about this devoted divorced couple, their new partners, and their two glib offspring at holiday time. It moves from a Currier and Ives winter wonderland of Christmas Eve in Connecticut to a New Year's Eve in sun-drenched Beverly Hills, California. It concerns the ex-marital couple, their lovers and would-be-lovers entering and exiting in a farcical, light-hearted, but deadserious comedy in two acts. There is no facile resolution to the question of "will-they-orwon't-they?" get back together. Rather, there is the emotional vitality of people clinging to what relational lifeboats they are tossed in the buoyant excursion called life!

OTHER TITLES AVAILABLE FROM SAMUEL FRENCH

CAPTIVE
Jan Buttram

Comedy / 2m, 1f / Interior

A hilarious take on a father/daughter relationship, this off beat comedy combines foreign intrigue with down home philosophy. Sally Pound flees a bad marriage in New York and arrives at her parent's home in Texas hoping to borrow money from her brother to pay a debt to gangsters incurred by her husband. Her elderly parents are supposed to be vacationing in Israel, but she is greeted with a shotgun aimed by her irascible father who has been left home because of a minor car accident and is not at all happy to see her. When a news report indicates that Sally's mother may have been taken captive in the Middle East, Sally's hard-nosed brother insists that she keep father home until they receive definite word, and only then will he loan Sally the money. Sally fails to keep father in the dark, and he plans a rescue while she finds she is increasingly unable to skirt the painful truths of her life. The ornery father and his loveable but slightly-dysfunctional daughter come to a meeting of hearts and minds and solve both their problems.